NO

NO

BUILDING A LIFE OF CHOICE
WITHOUT OBLIGATION

Darren Finkelstein
THE ACCOUNTABILITY GUY®

GRATITUDE AND APPRECIATION

Suzi (my bride of 40 years)
Jeremy and Hugh,
Adam and Karla,
and my grand-dog Nelson (good boy).

This book is dedicated to all of you.

Our family love has reinforced my strengths.
Reminding me that the essence of our existence together
and saying 'NO' to the chaos of our daily lives
is to make space as a family,
especially at Welshmans Reef, my 'happy place'.

Onward to the goldfields.
PS: Hurry up you lot, and please be on time, there's much to do!

Mum and Dad, I miss you both.
I know you are very proud of me.
You have always been my biggest fans.

'Sell. Sell. Sell.'
– yes, Dad, I'm on it.

Discover freedom of choice – start with 'NO'.

Darren Finkelstein

Results always matter

Here's what my accomplished and successful clients have achieved from our coaching sessions together. *You too could be enjoying this type of success.*

'One of the highlights of 2023 for me is that we started to work together. I am so happy and grateful for all your help and advice, and I'm so happy for the progress we are making together. I have full trust in your method and help, and I'm very confident we will achieve our goals together.'

Professor Selma Saidi – Technische Universität Braunschweig

'The best Accountability Coach in the game.'

Andrew Griffiths – international bestselling author and speaker

'We've worked with Darren for over five years. He has been a significant part of our business growth in that time. He is always encouraging and supportive, and provides wise advice. He also helped us successfully navigate the chaos of the COVID years. I highly recommend Darren if you want help taking your business to the next step.'

Michael Hanrahan – Publish Central

'After an incredibly challenging 18-month hiatus from our business due to our child's cancer treatment, returning to our professional life seemed almost insurmountable. That's when we found our extra-ordinary accountability coach, Darren, who not only understood the delicacy of our situation but also provided the precise motivation and assistance we desperately needed.'

Carly Saunders and Tresne Middleton – Teacher Professional Development

'My small business has grown three times in both staff and revenue in the time I've been working with Darren. This could not have been possible without him. His ability to get me to think big while being incredibly methodical and realistic about the steps needed to move forward have been the major catalyst for our growth. I could not have dreamed to be in this position two years ago. Darren is my secret weapon. I cannot recommend him highly enough.'

Scott Brown – Rural and Remote First Aid

'One of the world's leading accountability coaches.'

Callum Laing – investor/entrepreneur, Veblen Director Programme

'Can't say enough good things about Darren. He has helped me out of a long period of "stuckness" by providing advice, motivation and practical systems tailored to my particular requirements. I look forward to our sessions and always come out ready to go!'

Daniel McKinnon – Frontside Future

'I have had the pleasure of working with Darren for a couple of years now, and I cannot recommend his services highly enough. Darren has always had a different angle for consideration in all that we do together. His guidance is truly irreplaceable.'

Stephanie Rohde – PsychNEXUS

'Darren is an A-grade accountability coach. With a firm hand and a warm heart, he has helped me climb many mountains that might otherwise never have been achieved. I love working with him to tick those boxes!'

Tracy Angwin – Australian Payroll Association

'Darren has the ability to get you to focus on what is important (which means saying NO more often) and then complete those priority steps required for your business.'

Adam Burstin – Adbur Bookkeeping

'I had a fabulous session with Darren. Although I'm a seasoned business owner, Darren was able to unpack my business and show me some areas I could hone and where I was leaving revenue on the table. He's great at cutting through the overwhelm to get to the heart of the problem and then finding a fast, efficient solution. I fully recommend him for any business.'

Mari Williams – leadership coach, therapist and conflict mediator

MORE CLIENT SUCCESS STORIES

To watch my client success videos and read all of my reviews, scan this QR code.

First published in 2024 in Australia by Darren Finkelstein
The Accountability Guy®, founder of Tick Those Boxes Australia
M: +61 418 379 369
E: df@tickthoseboxes.com.au
Facebook: darren.finkelstein
LinkedIn: Darren Finkelstein
Instagram: @darren.finkelstein
www.tickthoseboxes.com.au
www.NOthebook.com.au

A catalogue entry for this book is available from the National Library of Australia.

ISBN: 978-1-923225-06-0

Project management and text design by Publish Central
Author photo: Kosta Iatrou (IKON Images)
Edited by Michael Hanrahan at Publish Central
Typeset by Kerry Milin at Production Works
Proudly printed in Australia by Pegasus Media & Logistics
Cover design by Julia Kuris
Illustrations: Jaroslav (Jaro) Jakovlev from Kharkiv, Ukraine (www.mistograf.com)

Other titles from Darren Finkelstein

The Accountability Advantage:
Play your best game
Release date: 01/02/2021; revised edition 01/10/23
ISBN: 978-1-92300749-9

Honey, let's buy a BOAT!
Boat ownership – Everything you wanted to know about buying (and selling)
a powerboat but didn't know who to ask
Release date: 01/10/2012
ISBN: 978-0-9873760-0-8

Honey, let's go BOATING!
101 bucket list of boating destinations
(Victorian edition)
Release date: 01/10/2014
ISBN: 978-0-9873760-2-2

Honey, let's sell the BOAT!
Finding the right buyer at the right price – 9 practical steps
Release date: 01/2/2016
ISBN: 978-0-9873760-5-3

Contents

Foreword

Learning to say 'NO' changed my life

One of the greatest lessons I've learned during my 40-plus years as an entrepreneur is that success isn't just about the things we do; it's also about the things we don't do. And, in many instances, what we don't do is even more important. That's why I loved being asked to write this foreword for my good friend and author Darren Finkelstein's latest book, which is all about empowering you to say 'NO'.

Throughout my early life, I struggled with having the courage to say 'NO'.

I struggled in my personal life as much as in my business life. I always felt I was doing everything for everyone else, and somewhere in between this and this, I got lost. The more I struggled to say 'NO', the more lost I became. Some of this was about self-worth, some was simply the need to give people pleasure (the two are, of course, connected), and sometimes I simply felt a responsibility to say 'YES'.

My strategy up until that point had been avoidance – trying to avoid the circumstances where I would be put on the spot and forced to say 'YES'. This meant avoiding people, which is not a very good strategy to go through life with. I reached a crossroads where I knew I had to change. I knew I had to learn how to say 'NO' in a way that made me feel okay.

And I did.

Slowly but surely, things started to change. I felt less resentful, I felt more in control, I got more of what mattered done, and I developed more self-respect. I also noticed that others treated me differently. They respected my ability to say 'NO'. They appreciated how I did it respectfully and in such a considerate way. This was a win–win for everyone.

Once I became more comfortable saying 'NO', my focus was clear, my commitment to myself and those closest to me was better defined, and my boundaries were sharper. I also started to achieve a great deal more. That's when I started to write books (14 bestsellers later), and I built my business, my brand, and a global reputation as a business leader.

None of this would have happened if I hadn't taken control of my life and learned to say 'NO' when I needed to and, even more importantly, when I *wanted* to.

Imagine what could happen in your life if you were comfortable saying 'NO' when you needed to and when it mattered to you. One thing I guarantee is that if you follow Darren's advice, particularly when he challenges you, and you learn to master the art of saying 'NO', every part of your life will feel more authentic, more connected and more engaged. You will feel far less frustrated, less like everyone else controls your life, and more empowered to do the things that are important to you.

I would also like to add that, having known Darren for a long time and worked closely with him, he talks the talk and walks the walk. He has the strength of character to say 'NO' when he needs to and when he wants to. He has his process, his tools and his philosophy, each of which he will share in this wonderful book.

You might think I'm being a little clichéd by saying I think this book is life-changing. But learning how to say 'NO' changed my life in extraordinary ways. Why couldn't it do the same for you? Imagine what you could achieve if you took control of every aspect of your life.

Reading this book is not just a step in the right direction; it's a mighty leap.

So, strap in, prepare to be challenged, stick to the path, and be ready to evolve in ways that will surprise and delight you.

Master the art of 'NO' and I guarantee you will forge the most extraordinary life.

Here's to embracing the power of saying 'NO'.

Andrew Griffiths
International bestselling author and global speaker

Embracing 'NO'

In a world that glorifies 'YES', the power of 'NO' remains underappreciated. 'YES' is seen as the key to opportunities, the door to new experiences, and the hallmark of cooperative, agreeable personalities. But what if we viewed 'NO' not as a refusal of an offer but as a profound assertion of choice, a declaration of value, and a cornerstone of personal empowerment?

This book – 'NO': Building a life of choice without obligation – is an exploration of that idea. Together, we will dig deep to better understand why we humans make so many 'YES' decisions without consideration of what truly best suits us, and we'll explore why humans from all walks of life don't respond favourably to hearing a 'NO' – even when a 'NO' is likely to be the better choice for them and you.

'Yeah-nah'

As Aussies, we often hear – and some of us use – the phrase 'YEAH-NAH', which at first glance seems contradictory but is steeped in nuance and cultural context. In essence, 'yeah-nah' is used to acknowledge what someone has said but simultaneously signal disagreement or a decision not to participate. It's an informal way of saying 'NO' that softens the refusal, making it more palatable and less direct.

The phrase 'yeah-nah' encapsulates a very Australian approach to communication, where understatement and affable roundabout ways of speaking are preferred over blunt directness. This linguistic pattern aligns with a cultural tendency to avoid confrontation and maintain a friendly social atmosphere, even when declining or disagreeing.

'Yeah-nah' speaks to this book's main theme of choice, and has a legitimate claim to be explored in depth. The phrase itself is an exercise in choice, reflecting the speaker's decision to acknowledge what's been said ('yeah') while also choosing to assert their own stance or decision ('nah') – a definitive 'NO'. It's a verbal embodiment of the delicate dance between social acknowledgement and personal choice.

That response, 'yeah-nah', to any question has always struck a chord with me – all the way back to the days I spent playing junior footy in the primary school yard with my buddies some 50 years ago. I still retain a clear memory like it was yesterday, especially when it came to the selection of teams. Even though I was excited to play with other under-12 kids, I wasn't very good at footy. So much so that the captain would often shout 'YEAH' to possibly having me on his team, followed by a quick 'NAH' when he realised I would hardly make a meaningful contribution to his team's efforts. It was pretty sad for me – it always hurt to be left out. I was a good team player; for me, the team always comes first, so I also sympathised with the captain's call to look after the best interests of the team to win the match. I understood why the other choices would offer greater benefit to the team, and much more value than my selection.

I have always appreciated the role of the captain, an on-field leader much like the CEO, who sees the importance of prioritising winning over all other considerations, even in the under-12s. After all, that is the main objective of team sports, right?

Besides, I wasn't much of a football player until I was in my late teens, when I finally had my growth spurt. I always gave it my all, but I was short and skinny, not ideal for an Australian Rules footballer.

Today, saying or hearing 'yeah-nah' gives me a sense of immense pleasure and a feeling of empowerment. To me, hearing 'yeah-nah' indicates the individual has found their voice. I've been thinking a lot about what makes that expression so characteristically Australian – a wonderful language construct that perfectly captures the people of Australia's informal, laid-back communication style.

The use of 'yeah-nah' also subtly speaks to the refusal to be bound by obligation. I, like so many other Aussies, commonly use the phrase in everyday interactions to navigate social obligations with a gentle refusal that's in line with my book's message of empowerment through saying 'NO'.

The difficulties in saying 'NO'

Nearly 50 years after those early school days, I work closely with business owners, managers, individuals and their teams from all around the world in my accountability coaching programs. We usually spend a lot of time going over past decisions and attempting to reverse what has already been done – when saying 'YES' seemed the easiest course of action but choosing to say 'NO' with respect and empathy would have been the better option. I've come to the realisation that I wish more of my clients and the community at large would initially say 'NO' more often. We tend to talk about this a lot; in fact, their capacity to say 'NO' and know when to delegate tasks to their team are arguably the most discussed topics among my clients. Some describe themselves as 'people-pleasers' who are unable or unconfident in their abilities to say 'NO'. A few acknowledge they say 'YES' to far too many things, much too frequently. They contend that saying 'YES' is far simpler than saying 'NO'. This is what inspired me to write this book: to better understand the common difficulties in saying 'NO', and to help people learn how to do so.

Imposter syndrome, self-doubt and lack of confidence are also reasons experienced by many. These are cases where even a solid, legitimate reason to say 'NO' is not going to work. Some people really need professional advice to help them move forward. Some could do with seeking counselling and others a psychologist. Perhaps a competent registered accountant to organise their tax returns and clear several years of backlog with the Australian Taxation Office will help.[1] Some could get enormous value from professional financial planning, and there are always those who require legal counsel, which is why having a capable solicitor on side is essential. Then there are those who

---

1   Please read the disclaimer on page 229.

simply require some marital counselling to better work together with their life partners, who are often also their business partners or on their team.

For me, I'm merely a street-smart entrepreneur with strong values, and a really good hunter who understands the importance and significance of rock-solid techniques.[2] While I am not formally qualified – after all, I am a high school dropout, and extremely proud of it – I do have a stellar reputation for integrity and an impressive track record of career, business and lifetime accomplishments. Along the way, yep, I've written a few best-selling books (five, including this one) and spent eight fun-filled years on talkback radio (3AW, for Melbourne readers) as the presenter of the Beach 'N' Bay reports live to air each summer.

When I should have said 'NO'

I was expelled from high school at the age of 17 and so had to dive into the workforce. I didn't have much of a choice: get a job or don't eat. I've done pretty well in the end, but my career path hasn't been all beer and skittles.

I have experienced my fair share of broken dreams and upsets, along with incredibly hard lessons and corporate scars, but all were wonderfully character-building. The saying 'what does not kill me only makes me stronger' certainly applies. I learnt about life firsthand, not from textbooks but from the school of hard knocks. These lessons taught me valuable life skills and built my resilience and street smarts, and gave me an opportunity to fine-tune my 'never say die' attitude. I feel it is my choice as to whether I sink or swim.

My rite of passage – from which I still proudly wear battle scars – was in my late 20s, having an entrepreneurial business not work out, and for things to go pear-shaped and into administration on Christmas Eve, putting off 10 staff and shutting my doors.

I often reflect and feel like I'm in good company. A tonne of successful entrepreneurs have had a business fail and lost everything. I did some research on successful business leaders

---

2   Please read the disclaimer on page 229.

who failed before, and found a great LinkedIn post by Dr Jayant Kumar (PhD). The student roll is mighty impressive:

- ☒ *Akio Morita*, who co-founded Sony. Due to low sales of a rice cooker that frequently burned the rice, Akio Morita's firm originally failed. He learned important lessons about quality control and customer expectations from this early loss, which he successfully utilised when co-founding Sony.

- ☒ *Bill Gates*, before building his empire, started a business called Traf-O-Data which went nowhere, and he dropped out of Harvard.

- ☒ *Colonel Sanders*'s famous secret chicken recipe was rejected over 1000 times before a restaurant accepted it. He founded KFC when he was 62 years old.

- ☒ *Evan Williams*, before co-founding the social media giant Twitter, started a company called Odeo, an unsuccessful podcasting platform.

- ☒ *Henry Ford*'s first two car companies failed and left him broke.

- ☒ *Mark Cuban*, before making billions selling his company to Yahoo, failed at a variety of jobs.

And last but by no means least ...

- ☒ *Richard Branson*. Even one of the richest people in the UK didn't get to where he is without a few failures along the way. Along with his famous Virgin Records and Virgin Airlines, he also developed Virgin Cola and Virgin Vodka, both of which failed.

And there's *Darren Finkelstein* – yes, me. My very first business ended in administration and receivership. In 1989, at the young age of 27, my wife, Suzi, and I watched the ANZ Bank sell our home to repay our debt of $500,000. That's an awful lot of money, and even more in today's terms. I'll share the full story in later chapters, because it's a perfect example of when I should have said 'NO' instead of a painful and very costly 'YES', which changed the course of my family's lives.

Why is 'NO' so powerful?

In researching this book and talking with many people, I've noticed a collective agreement that when someone says 'NO', someone else is losing out on a 'YES'. That is true, and occasionally a 'YES' is appropriate. However, I believe we don't discuss 'NO' enough. It's about having the agency to decide how to respond, rather than feeling obligated to fulfil every request or expectation by saying 'YES'.

Why is 'NO' so powerful? At its core, 'NO' is the ultimate expression of an individual's sovereignty. Each time we say 'NO', we are, in essence, declaring that we understand our limits, recognise our values, and are willing to stand by them. It's a testament to self-awareness and self-respect. In business and life, the ability to say 'NO' is not just about rejecting something unwanted; it's about affirming something else – something that, for us, holds greater value. Saying 'NO' is not a rejection; it's a strategic choice that can lead to positive outcomes for personal development, professional growth and overall life satisfaction.

However, saying 'NO' is not always as easy as it sounds. Social pressures, fear of missing out, guilt, and a plethora of other factors often cloud our judgement. We find ourselves saying 'YES' to things that drain our energy, divert our focus and detract from our larger goals. This habit of an automatic 'YES' can leave us overcommitted, resentful and burned out. Often, it's someone else's priorities that we are supporting, rather than our own.

In this book, I delve into the nuances of saying 'NO'. We will explore its history and psychological underpinnings, its impact on personal and professional relationships, and its role in shaping a balanced, fulfilling life. You'll learn not just *why* 'NO' is a powerful tool but also *how* to wield it effectively and compassionately and build a life of choice, without obligation. We will also confront the challenges and fears associated with saying 'NO'.

From fear of conflict to worries about missed opportunities, we'll tackle the common barriers that prevent people from embracing their ability to choose. Through practical advice, real-life examples and actionable strategies, this book will transform your relationship with 'NO'.

'NO' is not a word of rejection but a statement of prioritisation

By the end of this journey, you will see 'NO' in a new light. It is not a word of rejection but a statement of prioritisation, and a very positive, self-assured step forward – not backwards, as some might believe. It is not a closing door but a gateway to true self-fulfilment. It's not about limitation; it's about liberation.

Why is this liberation so important to me? Well, that's a darn good question!

I see and hear every day from my international accountability coaching and mentoring clients that there is a direct correlation between saying 'NO' and personal accountability. Of course there is.

In my book *The Accountability Advantage: Play your best game*, I wrote about emphasising the power of accountability in achieving personal and business goals. I introduced a straightforward, seven-step framework called 'The Road to Accountability', designed to significantly increase the likelihood of attaining goals, completing tasks and keeping commitments. By mastering accountability, individuals and organisations can experience substantial growth and success, moving from feeling overwhelmed to being in control and reaching new heights of achievement. The key message is that accountability is a superpower, vital for progress and fulfilment.

Being accountable helps you make deliberate decisions about your commitments and how they fit with your values and objectives. An extension of this idea is saying 'NO'. It entails selecting your responsibilities carefully and making sure they don't take you away from your goals, both personal and professional.

In the many years I have coached and mentored entre-preneurs, including managers, company owners, shareholders, boards and their teams, a pattern has become apparent: when it comes to certain decisions, saying 'NO' was the right one at the time, and if it had only been done sooner, a great deal of time, money and energy would have been saved. My story is a great example of that.

The accountability process is designed to facilitate personal and professional growth. Saying 'NO' to obligations that don't serve your growth or align with your values is a way of ensuring your actions are always contributing to your development.

The result of this is to reduce stress, overwhelm and over-commitment. Feeling overwhelmed and overcommitted can destroy self-confidence and self-belief, rendering you paralysed and unable to move forward as procrastination fogs your mind. Learning to say 'NO' helps in managing your workload, reducing stress and preventing burnout, thereby creating a more balanced and fulfilling life.

Saying 'NO' complements my principles and teachings of accountability by ensuring that your commitments are in alignment with your goals, values and priorities, enhancing your ability to live a life of choice without obligation. This leads to a more focused, balanced and ultimately successful personal and professional life.

In a culture that often equates busyness with productivity and success, saying 'NO' becomes an act of courage. It means you are willing to forgo immediate gratification or external valid-ation in favour of something more meaningful and aligned with your true purpose. This level of accountability extends beyond personal gain; it influences the quality of your interactions, the integrity of your commitments and the impact you have on those around you. Accountability through 'NO' also fosters authenticity. It encourages you to live a life true to yourself, not one dictated by others' expectations or societal norms.

Diverse perspectives are also necessary to foster creativity in the workplace and prevent division. Diversity can encourage thorough investigation, lead to better decisions and disprove assumptions. Teams that properly address these different opinions not only enhance their decision-making processes but also foster a more resilient and inclusive culture.

More creative thinking, improved team dynamics and increased personal and professional development are created in this setting, which results in more devoted and engaged team members. In any organisation, these dynamics are critical to innovation and attaining exceptional results.

Delivering 'NO' with respect and empathy

In a society where demands and responsibilities frequently overwhelm us, it's critical to acknowledge the enormous impact of the straightforward word 'NO'. The expression 'NO is a complete sentence' captures the notion that you don't have to provide an explanation or justification for your boundaries. I get the idea behind this statement, which empowers you to make decisions based on your needs, priorities and wellbeing, but I've never been a big admirer of the idea or the strictness of saying a black-and-white and potentially harsh 'NO'.

I feel that 'NOs' need careful and considered explanations delivered with honesty and empathy, so they provide clarity and foster understanding. When we take the time to explain our reasons for saying 'NO', we show respect for the person making the request. This helps maintain trust and builds stronger relationships by demonstrating that our decision is not a dismissal of the person but a thoughtful choice based on our priorities and boundaries.

Explaining our 'NO' allows us to communicate our values and limits clearly, ensuring that others understand our perspective and the rationale behind our decisions. This can prevent misunderstandings and reduce potential resentment, making it easier for others to accept and respect our choices. It also opens the door for dialogue and negotiation where necessary, allowing for more collaborative and mutually beneficial outcomes.

By delivering our 'NO' with respect and empathy, we acknowledge the other person's needs and feelings while staying true to our own. This balanced approach not only preserves relationships but also reinforces our commitment to living a life of choice and intentionality, where every decision is made with care and consideration. It's all in the delivery. We'll address this throughout the book.

Saying 'NO' – and incorporating my principles, framework and checklists into your life – will help you build a life of choice without obligation.

It's okay for you to say 'NO' to this concept, especially if you do not agree with this. Hold onto that 'NO' as you read on – your journey has just begun ... Your time will not be wasted as you open your mind to a different perspective that may just resonate.

Enjoy the read.

Onward to the goldfields.

THE ACCOUNTABILITY GUY ®

PART I

THE PSYCHOLOGY AND HISTORY OF 'NO'

Chapter 1

The power of 'NO'

In an era when there are more demands on our time and energy, the ability to say 'NO' has become more important than ever. The concept of choice vs duty is critical to our personal and professional fulfilment, but it remains one of the most difficult principles to continuously follow in our lives. I see this book, *NO: Building a life of choice without obligation*, as a beacon for individuals who want to negotiate the difficulties of modern responsibilities with integrity and meaning.

To set the scene, I want to look at the complex power of 'NO', including its psychological, social and practical ramifications. We will go through a tapestry of research, expert views and real-world examples to discover how a simple two-letter word can transform our way of life.

The word 'NO' is frequently connected with pessimism, rejection and squandered opportunities. However, when used deliberately and with consideration, 'NO' can be a powerful instrument for creating a life of choice rather than obligation. Let's get to the heart of expressing 'NO' effectively, investigating its rationale, confronting limiting assumptions, and uncovering the transformative benefits it has for both personal and professional lives.

Rationales for saying 'NO'

As social creatures and business professionals, we are constantly besieged with requests. Meetings, projects, family commitments and social responsibilities compete for our limited time and energy. Saying 'NO' does not represent rudeness or ungratefulness; rather, it reflects strategic resource allocation. Declining requests on a personal level can be difficult, especially when juggling relationships with family and friends or social expectations. Understanding the rationale for saying 'NO' can empower you to make intentional decisions that prioritise your wellbeing and encourage healthy interactions.

Let's take a deeper look at the possible reasons for denying personal requests:

- ☒ **Establishing boundaries.** Your physical and emotional reserves are used up with each 'YES'. Saying 'NO' more often helps you save energy for the things and people that truly matter in your life. For every one of us, time and space are finite resources. By learning to say 'NO', you can set priorities for your time that align with your values and create time for relaxation, self-care and personal growth.

- ☒ **Maintaining your beliefs and aspirations.** Not all requests correspond with your values and goals. Saying 'NO' to misaligned activities allows you to stay loyal to yourself and your goals.

- ☒ **Building healthy relationships.** Respectful relationships that are honest and based on trust are strengthened by effective communication of boundaries and preferences. Healthy relationships must be transparent.

- ☒ **Answering 'YES' frequently can result in unhealthy relationships that breed anger, resentment and tiredness.** Reciprocity and a willingness to share are essential for happy relationships. Relying too much on you also doesn't educate the other person on how to stand on their own two feet, acquire new skills, learn and expand their thinking, or take ownership and responsibility for themselves.

Saying 'NO' does not represent rudeness or ungratefulness; rather, it reflects strategic resource allocation.

Darren Finkelstein

☒ **Refusing a request with assertiveness and not rudeness shows respect for oneself.** It is a powerful demonstration of self-respect and can indeed inspire others to adopt a similar approach.

There are also deeper rationales behind the choice to decline a request, which are multifaceted. Here are my top six:

1 **Preservation of self:** Every person has finite time, energy and emotional bandwidth. Saying 'NO' protects these resources and ensures that we don't deplete ourselves to the point of bunout.

2 **Prioritisation:** By saying 'NO' to certain requests, we can say 'YES' to things that matter more to us. This allows us to focus on what truly aligns with our goals and passions.

3 **Authenticity:** When we say 'YES' out of obligation, we are not being true to ourselves. Declining requests that do not resonate with us fosters authenticity and ensures that our actions are in harmony with our true self.

4 **Respect for others:** Ironically, saying 'NO' can also be a form of respect for others. It prevents situations where we might do a poor job because our hearts aren't in it. By being honest, we allow the other party to find someone who is genuinely willing and able to fulfill the request.

5 **Setting a precedent:** How we respond to requests sets expectations for future interactions. Saying 'NO' establishes a precedent that our time and choices are valuable and not to be taken lightly.

6 **Growth and development:** Finally, when we decline opportunities that are not right for us, we leave room for growth and new experiences that are better suited to our journey. This selective process is essential for personal development.

The art of saying 'NO' is not about negativity; it is about making conscious choices. It is about choosing to live intentionally rather than reactively. Each 'NO' is a stepping stone towards a life built on deliberate decisions.

Frequently held beliefs about 'NO'

The power of saying 'NO' extends beyond the mere act of refusal; it's a profound exercise in personal autonomy and integrity. It's about the liberation that comes from being able to set and honour your own boundaries. Far from being a mere negative response, 'NO' is an essential aspect of personal dialogue – a conversation between your inner self and the external demands of the world.

Frequently, 'NO' is saddled with negative connotations, a residue of societal beliefs and expectations. Let's explore some of these beliefs and the empowering truths behind the power of NO':

Belief: 'NO' is hostile or rude.

Truth: 'NO' is an assertion of personal space. It communicates self-respect and respect for the needs and limits of others. It is not an act of hostility but one of honest communication.

Belief: 'NO' indicates selfishness.

Truth: 'NO' is often an act of self-care. It's about recognising your limits and not overcommitting – a necessary step in maintaining mental, emotional and physical health.

Belief: 'NO' means you're not a team player.

Truth: Saying 'NO' can support teamwork by ensuring that when you commit, you do so with full engagement. It's about quality over quantity in terms of contribution.

Belief: 'NO' shuts down opportunities.

Truth: 'NO' can open the door to the right opportunities. It means you're making space for choices that truly resonate with your values and goals, rather than filling life with distractions.

Belief: 'NO' is a sign of weakness.

Truth: It takes strength and courage to say 'NO'. It's easy to give in to pressure, but it requires fortitude to stand firm in one's decisions.

Belief: 'NO' is negative and creates conflict.

Truth: 'NO' can be one of the most positive things you say because it can prevent resentment and burnout. When used constructively, it can steer relationships and situations away from potential conflict.

Belief: 'NO' is final and absolute.

Truth: 'NO' can be flexible. It can mean 'not now' or 'not in this way'. It can be a starting point for negotiation and finding mutually agreeable solutions.

Belief: 'NO' will hurt your relationships.

Truth: While true in unhealthy, co-dependent relationships, genuine connections respect boundaries and understand the need to decline and compromise sometimes. Clear communication and offering alternatives can further minimise any negative impact.

Belief: 'NO' means you have a closed mind.

Truth: This one is close to my heart as I've discussed this in numerous client sessions, hence the length of my response. Saying 'NO' is often mistakenly perceived as an indication of a closed and negative mind because of prevalent social expectations and cultural norms that value agreeableness and compliance. This perception is rooted in the belief that saying 'YES' is inherently positive and accommodating, while 'NO' is seen as negative or uncooperative. However, this oversimplification overlooks the nuanced rationale behind the choice to decline. In reality, saying 'NO' is not a marker of negativity or closed-mindedness but can be a conscious choice that stems from a place of self-awareness and thoughtful consideration.

In this book, I will be embracing the opportunity to challenge these misconceptions and highlight the positive, life-affirming aspects of saying 'NO'. By empowering you to say 'NO' without guilt, I am encouraging you to live with intentionality, to make choices that enrich your life, and to engage with the world on your terms. Through this lens, 'NO' becomes not just a word, but a philosophy for living with authenticity and purpose.

'NO' can be a positive and open-minded response

Responding 'YES' as a default reaction, as often promoted by well-meaning counsel from parents or friends, is not necessarily the best approach. Neglecting one's own needs and limits can result from continuously granting others' requests, which goes against self-care and setting boundaries, often enabling the 'people-pleasing' mindset. You must strike a balance between looking out for others and taking care of yourself.

A 'people-pleaser' is someone who goes to great lengths to make others happy, often at the expense of their own needs or desires. People-pleasers frequently find it difficult to say 'NO' or establish personal boundaries. Their behaviour may be driven by a need to be liked and respected, a fear of rejection or a dispute. Though being kind and flexible can be good qualities, going overboard with people-pleasing can impede personal development and authenticity in relationships in addition to causing stress, exhaustion and resentment.

Resentment and burnout are the results of over-commitment, a common consequence of habitual people-pleasing. This not only affects your mental and emotional health but can also negatively impact the quality of the work or help provided. True friends and loved ones will understand and respect your need for self-care.

Here are some reasons why 'NO' can be a positive and open-minded response, not a negative one:

- ☒ **Self-awareness:** It indicates a strong sense of self and a clear understanding of values, limits and priorities. It shows you have thoughtfully considered the request and determined that it does not align with your personal or professional goals.

- ☒ **Healthy boundaries:** Declining an offer is often a sign of having healthy boundaries. It's about recognising your capacity and refusing to overcommit.

- ☒ **Focused commitment:** Saying 'NO' allows you to commit fully to current engagements. It's about quality over quantity.

- ☒ **Strategic decision-making:** A 'NO' can be a strategic decision that stems from an understanding of your goals and the most effective path to achieve them. It's about making choices that best serve your objectives.

- ☒ **Opportunity for others:** When you decline opportunities that are not a good fit for you, you leave room for others who may be better suited or more passionate about those opportunities.

- ☒ **Positive reorientation:** A 'NO' can redirect energy and resources towards more fulfilling endeavours. It creates space for opportunities that are more aligned with your aspirations.

- ☒ **Constructive feedback:** A well-reasoned 'NO' can provide valuable feedback. It can highlight issues that may need to be addressed and encourage others to refine their requests or offers.

- ☒ **Authentic relationships:** Saying 'NO' contributes to building more authentic and transparent relationships, both personally and professionally, by setting clear expectations.

- ☒ **Empowerment:** By saying 'NO', you empower yourself to take control of your life and make active choices, rather than passively acquiescing to the will of others.

- ☒ **Adaptability:** Far from being a sign of closed-mindedness, the ability to say 'NO' can demonstrate adaptability – knowing when to change course and when to stay true to your path is a vital life skill.

Saying 'NO' – when done judiciously and for the right reasons – reflects an open-mindedness to your own needs and wellbeing, a positive intention to fulfil commitments with integrity, and the strategic foresight to cultivate a life that resonates with your values. It is an essential component of building a life of choice without obligation.

Protecting your personal resources

Prioritising resources and goals leads to a life of choice, and saying 'NO' with absolute confidence hinges on managing your resources and goals effectively.

Prioritising your goals requires clarity and focus, which entails making sure you are spending enough time on the activities that are crucial to your success. Finding what matters is made easier with clarity and focus. You can purposefully manage your time, energy and resources to achieve your intended results by being aware of your priorities. This clarity provides a solid basis for your decision-making.

Knowing you have limited resources – money, time and energy – allows you to say 'NO' to situations that don't fit with your priorities, avoiding overload and ensuring you make the necessary investments in your objectives. You can stop 'chasing shiny objects' and other distractions.

Setting limits by creating boundaries also builds confidence. Prioritising your own goals strengthens your sense of direction and purpose. This makes it easier to set boundaries and politely decline requests that don't contribute to your aspirations.

Having awareness of the opportunity cost of each 'YES' is made easier by setting priorities for your goals. Saying 'YES' to anything entails saying 'NO' to something else. Knowing this trade-off can help you make deliberate decisions that will lead to the future you want. Knowing your resource limitations forces you to be selective about your commitments. When resources are scarce, you naturally become more cautious about saying 'YES', leading to a life built on intentional choices, not obligations.

Saying 'NO' confidently to things that don't align with your priorities frees up your mental and physical energy, allowing you to devote yourself fully to the things that do. It will also reduce stress and enhance your efficiency. Overload and burnout can be avoided by prioritising your own objectives and resources. This helps you concentrate on the things that truly matter, which lessens the tension and worry that comes with balancing too many obligations. You can pursue your goals with greater productivity and efficiency because of this mental clarity.

Don't let peer pressure make you say 'YES' to things you don't want to do.

Saying 'NO' when required shows respect for your time and yourself. This is where self-respect and personal integrity come in. It demonstrates your commitment to upholding your priorities over those of others. This cultivates honesty and self-assurance, enabling you to live life on your terms, and ensuring you're investing in what truly matters to you. This alignment between your actions and values fosters a sense of authenticity and integrity. (Setting priorities will be covered in later chapters.)

Managing risk

When you are comfortable saying 'NO', it is simpler to manage risk by making well-informed judgements since you can decide what to accept and what to decline. This gives you the confidence to decline choices that pose a high risk or have consequences that don't fit with your values or objectives.

Considerable benefits can result from taking measured risks. By being aware of potential dangers, you can compare prospective advantages against potential losses and make more thoughtful decisions. This enables you to accept chances with measured risks that fit within your risk tolerance while also saying 'NO' to careless ones. This protects your valuable resources, such as your time, energy, money and reputation. By avoiding unnecessarily risky commitments, you safeguard these resources for the things that truly matter to you.

Upholding your standards and principles is the key to maintaining quality in all spheres of your life. This gives you the confidence to turn down offers that don't live up to your expectations, allowing you to act on your priorities. Protecting your integrity is achieved by maintaining quality in your commitments and actions. You uphold your personal integrity and build trust with yourself and others. This allows you to say 'NO' with confidence, knowing you're staying true to your values and avoiding situations that could compromise your integrity.

Making sustainable choices comes from the ability to say 'NO' to low-quality commitments, ensuring you're not spreading yourself thin or sacrificing quality for quantity. This allows you to focus on high-quality pursuits that are more likely to be sustainable and fulfilling in the long run.

Saying 'NO' allows you to say 'YES' to what is truly important.

Darren Finkelstein

Managing risks and maintaining quality are crucial aspects of saying 'NO' and building a life of choice. By understanding and managing risks, you make informed decisions and protect your resources. By maintaining quality standards, you stay true to your values and build a life that aligns with your priorities.

Here are two examples of how managing risk and maintaining quality could be compromised:

- ☒ **A construction company receives an urgent request for a fast-tracked project with unclear safety regulations.** Saying 'NO' shields the organisation from legal and reputational threats, while prioritising employee safety and ethical practices.

- ☒ **A software development team rushes to launch a new feature without proper testing.** Saying 'NO' ensures quality control, preventing bugs and poor consumer feedback.

Remember, these are just two examples to illustrate the rationale for saying 'NO'. The specific reasons and situations will vary depending on your individual and organisational context. However, understanding the underlying principles of resource management, prioritisation and boundary setting can empower you to make informed decisions and navigate both personal and professional requests with confidence and clarity.

By broadening your understanding of the power of 'NO', you can create a life and profession in which saying 'NO' allows you to say 'YES' to what is truly important.

The generation gap

I'm proudly a Baby Boomer, and feel the old ways do reflect the generation gap. Jeez, now I sound like my parents but I feel that I've proudly earned my grey-haired wisdom (and there's not much hair left). Each grey hair was created as a result of the mistakes I've made, the wins I've celebrated, the losses that have brought me to tears, and those hard-fought debates with folks who do not see the world as I do ... and there's been a few of them.

Throughout my working career, I clearly remember instances where, upon suggesting that we respond with a 'NO' to certain requests, management would often use specific phrases in their replies. Reflecting on those phrases as I write, I realise how much I've evolved both personally and professionally. Fortunately, it's not just me that evolved, so have business practices, and our ways of communicating with clients have also undergone a significant transformation, much to my delight. This evolution has reshaped our understanding of client interactions and the importance of navigating requests and expectations with nuance and strategic insight.

Here are some of the classic lines from my old bosses, together with my current thinking, in *italics*. How wrong were they?

☒ **'If we say no to clients, it will damage our reputation.'**
I call BS on this statement because declining a request or opportunity can actually bolster a company's reputation when handled correctly. Saying 'NO' can signify a company's commitment to excellence, as it shows they are focusing on their strengths and delivering only what they can manage at their best quality and execution.
It also demonstrates a level of honesty and integrity, which can build trust with clients in the long run. By being transparent about capabilities and limits, businesses can set realistic expectations, prevent overpromising and underdelivering, and establish a reputation for reliability and professionalism. It's about saying 'NO' to the right things, at the right times, for the right reasons. This strategic selectivity ensures that when a company does say 'YES', it means they are fully committed to delivering on their promise, thereby strengthening client relationships and their own market standing.

☒ **'Saying no makes us appear weak.'** *I call BS on this because an organisation's ability to say 'NO' is actually a sign of strength and confidence. It shows that a business understands its value proposition and is focused on delivering quality services or products within its capacity. By setting clear boundaries and realistic expectations,* *companies can avoid overextension, which often leads to subpar outcomes and dissatisfied customers. A respectful and well-justified 'NO' can foster respect and credibility, as it assures clients that the business won't take on work that compromises its standards. In fact, this selectiveness can lead to stronger client relationships, as it underscores a commitment to excellence and establishes a foundation of trust.*

☒ **'Saying no goes against "hustle" culture.'** *I'm calling BS on this too because the true essence of the hustle is about working smarter, not just harder. It's about strategic alignment of one's efforts to ensure that every 'YES' is impactful and meaningful. Hustle culture, when properly channelled, isn't about saying 'YES' to everything, but rather about knowing when to say 'NO' to things that don't serve your mission or will divert resources from more critical tasks. In fact, the most successful hustlers know that to maintain momentum and to keep their operations lean and focused, they must be discerning in their commitments. It's this calculated decision-making process that propels sustained success, not the relentless grind at the expense of health, relationships and quality of work.*

☒ **'Saying no stifles innovation.'** *Tonnes of BS on this because it can actually have the opposite effect. Saying 'NO' to certain ideas or projects can free up resources and creative energy, allowing a focus on truly innovative work. It prevents spreading oneself too thin, which can dilute the creative process and lead to mediocre outcomes. By being selective, we create the space needed for deep work and the cultivation of truly groundbreaking ideas. It's not about shutting down creativity; it's about channelling it wisely.*

Incorporating this thinking into our interactions signifies a mature approach to communication, where clarity, respect and mutual understanding can prevail. It highlights the importance of being selective about commitments, which in turn allows for more meaningful, productive and sustainable engagements. Ultimately, building a life and business practice centred around choice without obligation enriches both personal wellbeing and professional integrity, fostering environments where both parties can thrive.

Building autonomy and self-determination: Taylor Swift

Taylor Swift's business acumen is marked by her strategic vision, keen sense of brand management and adeptness at leveraging her intellectual property.

Swift meticulously oversees her brand, carefully curating her image and the narrative surrounding her music and public persona. This includes taking a stand for artists' rights, most notably through her very public disputes with music streaming services over fair compensation and her decision to re-record her earlier albums to regain control over her master recordings. Her ability to say 'NO' and question the status quo is extraordinary.

This is underpinned by her proactive engagement with her fan base through social media and tailored marketing strategies significantly enhancing her brand's value and reach, exemplifying her sophisticated understanding of both the creative and commercial aspects of the music industry.

Swift's well-publicised intention to re-record her songs embraces a philosophy of 'NO'. And 'YES' I'm pleased to declare that I'm a Swiftie who is engrossed in the 2024 Eras World Tour at the time of writing this chapter.

Let's take a deep dive on Taylor Swift's decision to re-record her music as this serves as a compelling case study for 'building a life of choice without obligation'. This move is not merely a business strategy; it's a declaration of independence and a masterclass in navigating her career under her own terms:

- ☒ **Empowerment through choice.** Swift's action underscores the power of choice in a professional landscape. By choosing to re-record her albums, she demonstrated a refusal to be constrained by previous contracts and industry norms that do not serve the artist's interest. This decision highlights how empowerment stems from making choices that align with one's values and long-term vision.

- ☒ **Strategic use of 'NO'.** Swift's situation arose from her saying 'NO' to the status quo, where artists often have little control over their masters. This 'NO' is not just a rejection but a proactive stance against a traditional industry practice that she viewed as unjust. It's a powerful example of how saying 'NO' to unacceptable conditions can open up new avenues for creativity and control.

- ☒ **Navigating obligations.** Swift's approach to re-recording her music illustrates how obligations can be re-evaluated and renegotiated. Instead of accepting her lack of ownership as an unchangeable obligation, she took matters into her own hands, transforming her situation into one where she could dictate the terms.

- ☒ **Innovation and adaptation.** Swift's strategy was unprecedented in its scale within the music industry, showcasing how thinking outside traditional frameworks can lead to groundbreaking outcomes.

- ☒ **Personal and professional integrity.** Swift's decision was rooted in a deep sense of personal and professional integrity, aligning her actions with her principles.

- ☒ **Influence and impact.** Swift's journey has the potential to inspire not just artists but individuals in any field to consider how they might exercise more autonomy over their work and lives. Her impact extends beyond music, influencing conversations around artists' rights, intellectual property and the power dynamics of creative industries.

My key takeaway is Taylor Swift's decision to re-record her music wasn't just about the music itself; it was a powerful statement about reclaiming control, building a life of choice and inspiring others to do the same. It's a story that transcends the music industry and speaks to the universal desire for autonomy and self-determination.

Remember that you may just be dealing with frequently held beliefs, not universal truths. Challenge them and develop your understanding based on your personal context and values. By embracing 'NO' thoughtfully and responsibly, you pave the way for a more fulfilling and empowered life, both personally and professionally.

Staying focused on the big goals: Steve Jobs

Steve Jobs – co-founder of Apple Inc. in the 1990s – was my boss when I worked for Apple as the Manager of Commercial Markets in Australia from 1992 to 2002. Steve was renowned for his laser-like concentration and unwavering dedication to realising his vision of technology that is easy to use.

I used to visit Apple's headquarters – 1 Infinite Loop in Cupertino, California – and heard a lot from my colleagues about Steve's ability to say 'NO', and I witnessed it firsthand a few times myself. Any interruptions to Steve's plans for product development, on which he was completely focused, were his pet peeve. Being in his company could be unsettling because it was obvious when he thought an idea or concept being presented was absurd. He would lose his mind since he had no time for diversions or anything that might delay the company's goals. Tears frequently flowed when suggestions were made and Steve vehemently rejected them, often publicly berating and reducing the person to ashes.

Steve was known for placing a high value on quality and simplicity. Prototypes and concepts that fell short of his expectations or weren't in line with his vision for Apple were frequently dismissed as 'time-wasting distractions'.

This deliberate strategy was essential to Apple's creation of revolutionary devices like the iPhone, iMac and iPad, which completely changed the electronics industry. Apple was able to lead the industry in design and functionality thanks to Steve's emphasis on saying 'NO' to the unnecessary.

I found Steve's unstable temperament and constant personality changes really fascinating and rather scary, as I, like most other staff members, was not sure which version of Steve we'd get each day.

Steve's responses are famous, and there's a popular YouTube video capturing Steve saying an emphatic 'NO' called 'Focusing is About Saying No'. Use the QR code provided at the end of this section to watch and listen as Steve explains his thinking really

well and respectfully. Steve's response pretty much follows my 10-step framework in chapter 8. Nice one, Steve.

Listen carefully as Steve answers a brave audience member's question during Apple's 1997 Worldwide Developers Conference, which serves as a prime illustration of saying 'NO'. I was also lucky enough to be in attendance at this event.

The power of 'NO' in scientific focus and goal clarity: Professor Selma Saidi

It is impossible to exaggerate the importance of strategic concentration and goal clarity in the field of scientific research, where complicated issues call for creative answers. In this section, a renowned faculty leader at Germany's Technische Universität Braunschweig (TU Braunschweig), Professor Selma Saidi PhD., shares her observations. TU Braunschweig is Germany's oldest institute of technology, having been founded in 1745. It is also a proud member of TU9, an incorporated society of the most renowned and largest German institutes of technology, a tribute to its great legacy of distinction in engineering and sciences.

In my discussion with Professor Saidi, she sheds light on the often underestimated value of saying 'NO'. She says that every time she declines to participate in some activity or opportunity, she is saying 'YES' to priorities that are more closely aligned with her goals.

As she notes, the inability to say 'NO' is usually caused by a lack of clarity in objectives and a lack of focus. This realisation is especially relevant to the scientific community, which is known for its bright minds addressing some of the world's most important problems.

Professor Saidi's key point is that scientific work requires a laser-like focus. There are many possible distractions on the path to deciphering and resolving difficult situations. Although they are frequently alluring, these diversions can seriously take away from the main objective, diluting efforts and producing less-than-optimal results. Thus, having the ability to say 'NO' involves more than merely practising refusal; it also involves making a calculated choice to focus one's time, money and mental energy on projects that are most in line with one's main research objectives.

This idea of selected participation is further reinforced in the context of Professor Saidi's academic environment at TU Braunschweig by the historical and modern relevance of the university. The surroundings are full of possibilities and paths for investigation because they are at the forefront of scientific and technical development. But only the astute scientist, equipped with a clear understanding of their study aims, can successfully navigate this without losing sight of their ultimate objectives.

Professor Saidi's emphasis on the power of 'NO' in scientific focus and goal clarity highlights the significance of selective participation in advancing meaningful research and making academic breakthroughs. This is particularly important for 'moving the needle' in research.

Professor Saidi highlights the significance of the following crucial areas:

☒ **Setting resource priorities:** Resources like money, time and staff are frequently scarce. Saying 'NO' to less important topics or side pursuits allows academics to focus their limited resources on studies with the greatest potential for breakthroughs or substantial impact.

☒ **Enhanced focus:** To solve complicated issues and generate new theories, academic research necessitates intense concentration and lengthy periods of reflection. Rejecting extraneous activities enables researchers to focus more intently on their main areas of interest, improving the calibre and scope of their work.

☒ **Preventing overcommitment:** Academics are frequently under pressure to assume a variety of responsibilities, including teaching, administrative work, publishing, and more. Saying 'NO' when necessary can assist in avoiding overcommitting, which lowers stress and burnout. Maintaining long-term productivity and passion for their primary research endeavours depends on this energy conservation.

☒ **Strategic career management:** In academia, high-quality work is frequently more important than quantity for career advancement. Saying 'NO' to opportunities that do not fit with their strategic career goals allows academics to concentrate on important initiatives, networking and publication in high-impact journals that elevate their professional status.

☒ **Fostering innovation:** Innovation calls for not only a lot of effort but also the capacity for original thought and the willingness to challenge accepted wisdom. Researchers can provide unique insights and discoveries that really 'move the needle' by rejecting easy routes or projects that are broadly accepted and concentrating on unusual or riskier ideas.

☒ **Determining limits for equilibrium of work–life balance:** The ability to set boundaries effectively, including when to say 'NO', is essential for preserving a positive work–life balance. Maintaining this equilibrium is crucial for maintaining both one's health and the creative and intellectual energy required for advanced research.

☒ **Promoting a focused research agenda:** Researchers might create a more focused and cohesive research agenda by turning down side initiatives. Their status as authorities in a particular field is strengthened by this focus, which facilitates the recruitment of financing, partners and topnotch students.

According to Professor Saidi, being able to say 'NO' is a strategic instrument that is necessary for encouraging noteworthy academic achievements and expanding the boundaries of knowledge in the competitive and demanding world of academia.

Professor Saidi's observations not only provide a practical method for attaining research efficacy, but also capture a more general lesson in life about the significance of having the guts to set priorities, being held accountable for your actions and having clear goals, a message Professor Saidi tries to instil in her PhD students on a frequent basis.

Personally, I love the concept of 'moving the needle' in research, and I truly understand why it's so important to Professor Saidi, and her PhD students. It signifies making significant progress or breakthroughs that advance knowledge, solve critical problems and contribute substantively to the field of science.

For Professor Saidi and her peers, particularly at an institution as prestigious as TU Braunschweig, the ability to effect meaningful change through research is a core objective for several reasons:

- ☒ **Advancing knowledge:** In academia, the primary goal is to expand the body of knowledge within various disciplines. By 'moving the needle', researchers like Professor Saidi are not just contributing incremental knowledge; they are making groundbreaking discoveries that can redefine understanding in their fields.

- ☒ **Solving complex problems:** Many research projects aim to address some of the most pressing and complex issues facing society today. These could range from environmental challenges to health crises. Professor Saidi values the ability to say 'NO' to lesser distractions to concentrate resources and intellectual energy on projects that promise the most impactful solutions.

- ☒ **Innovation and creativity:** Scientific progress involves innovative thinking and novel approaches. For Professor Saidi, saying 'NO' to conventional or safe paths can free up mental space and resources to explore more creative or risky ideas that could lead to significant technological and scientific advancements.

- ☒ **Career and institutional prestige:** Success in making substantial research breakthroughs not only enhances the reputation of the individual researcher but also elevates the status of their institution. This, in turn, attracts more funding, better students and high-quality faculty members, creating a virtuous cycle of excellence and innovation.

☒ **Impact on policy and society:** Research that 'moves the needle' can influence policy decisions and have a direct impact on societal welfare. Researchers driven by the desire to make a difference in the real world see their work as a means to effect change and improve lives.

For Professor Saidi, the importance of impactful research lies in its capacity to generate significant and lasting contributions to science and society. Her focus on saying 'NO' is directly tied to this ambition, highlighting the strategic need to filter out distractions and deepen commitment to research that has the potential to change paradigms and improve human understanding and quality of life.

After all, they are our scientific futures, the professor says.

CHAPTER 1 REVIEW

My goal for this chapter was to debunk the myths that have long painted 'NO' in a negative light, revealing it instead as a fulcrum of autonomy, integrity and strategic resource allocation. I tried to be both incisive and empathetic, encouraging you to confront deeply rooted assumptions and embrace the act of refusal not as an obstruction but as a constructive and necessary declaration of self-respect.

Top takeaways and lessons learned

☒ **Self-preservation:** 'NO' is an essential tool for maintaining one's wellbeing, conserving energy for what truly matters.

☒ **Strategic prioritisation:** 'NO' enables us to focus on our values and passions, improving the quality of our engagement and work.

☒ **Assertive authenticity:** Saying 'NO' encourages us to remain true to our beliefs and aspirations, fostering a life of authenticity.

☒ **Constructive communication:** 'NO' enhances relationships through clear boundaries and mutual respect.

☒ **Empowerment:** Learning to say 'NO' empowers us to make deliberate decisions that align with personal growth and professional development.

☒ **Deconstructing negativity:** This chapter challenges misconceptions about 'NO' being negative, advocating for its role in fostering positive outcomes.

☒ **Generational evolution:** This chapter addresses the shift in mindset across generations regarding the power and perception of 'NO'.

☒ **Holistic application:** 'NO' is beneficial across various aspects of life, from personal wellbeing to professional integrity and societal change.

☒ **Cultural impact:** The chapter underscores the capacity of 'NO' to transcend individual interactions and influence broader societal norms and expectations.

Bonus takeaway

Listen to the words in Taylor's song 'Long Live' (Taylor's version). This is a song that celebrates the experiences, friendships and achievements she had during a specific era of her career. It is often associated with the 'Fearless' era. The song reflects on the journey, the challenges faced and the bonds formed during that time. In my opinion, the song honours all the occasions when she had to say 'NO' to uphold her morals, goals and dreams, staying true to her chosen course.

Chapter 2

'NO' through the ages

The historical and cultural views on refusing offers by saying 'NO' vary widely across different societies and periods. Allow me to take you on a fascinating historical tour to see how people have interpreted 'NO' through the ages. Understanding the past and how we got to where we are today helps, in my opinion, to understand in which direction we are headed.

The art of tactful refusal

In many ancient societies, such as Ancient Rome, Ancient Greece, The Celts, The Minoans and The Etruscans, hospitality was considered a sacred duty, and refusing an offer – for example, saying 'NO' to a meal – could be seen as an insult to the host. That still doesn't explain why my dear late mother Ruth always took it so personally. In ancient societies, saying 'NO' would have to be done with great tact to avoid offending. It's good to see that my key messages in this book were being implemented so many years ago.

In Confucian societies like ancient China, harmony was a key value, and direct refusal was often avoided in favour of more subtle, indirect methods of declining offers.

These ancient and classical perspectives on saying 'NO' inform modern understandings of building a life of choice without obligation.

Darren Finkelstein

In ancient Greece and Rome, the concept of hospitality, or 'xenia' in Greek, was more than just a social custom; it was an ethical imperative and often a religious duty. Guests were seen as under the protection of the gods, especially Zeus or Jupiter, who were considered the divine enforcers of hospitality. Therefore, to refuse an offer by saying 'NO' was not merely a personal slight to the host but a potential defiance of the will of the gods.

Therefore, indirect methods of declining offers were preferred, such as using polite excuses, suggesting alternatives, or even agreeing initially but then finding ways to non-confrontationally withdraw later. The goal was to navigate social situations in a manner that preserved relationships and maintained collective wellbeing. Saying 'NO' required careful negotiation to avoid damaging one's social standing and to respect the sacred nature of hospitality. It's interesting to note that in today's society, those same tactful refusal techniques and methodologies work just as effectively.

These ancient and classical perspectives on saying 'NO' inform modern understandings of building a life of choice without obligation. They highlight the importance of respecting social bonds while asserting personal choice. The ability to refuse effectively in a manner that is considerate of others' feelings and societal norms is a nuanced skill that balances individual freedom with collective harmony.

In today's globalised world, these historical nuances contribute to a more sophisticated approach to personal boundaries and the affirmation of choice – a strategy I fully endorse. Our goal is to enhance relationships by saying 'NO' with respect and empathy. (This goal forms a crucial part of my 10-step framework in chapter 8.)

Eastern and Western perspectives

Eastern cultures tend to emphasise group harmony and social cohesion. Therefore, refusing offers by saying 'NO' can sometimes be viewed as confrontational or disrespectful. It's common to find more indirect ways of refusing offers.

Western cultures, particularly in modern times, often value directness and individualism, so refusing offers by saying 'NO' can be seen as a straightforward expression of personal choice and boundaries.

The differences in how saying 'NO' is perceived and practised between Eastern and Western cultures largely stem from their divergent value systems and societal structures, which in turn shape individual behaviour and thought processes regarding autonomy and obligation.

Let's explore the different perspectives.

Eastern perspectives focus on:

☒ **Collectivism:** Eastern cultures typically emphasise collectivism, where the needs and goals of the group (family, community or society) often take precedence over individual desires. This cultural norm fosters an environment where saying 'NO' outright can be seen as a refusal to conform to the group's needs and a disruption of social harmony.

☒ **Indirect communication:** In many Eastern cultures, communication tends to be more indirect. The art of subtlety and reading context is crucial, as it allows individuals to decline offers or requests in a way that does not cause embarrassment or disharmony. This indirectness helps maintain relationships and 'face', a concept that refers to a person's reputation within the community.

☒ **Hierarchical structures:** Respect for elders and superiors is deeply ingrained in Eastern societies. The ability to refuse offers by saying 'NO' can be heavily influenced by one's position within the social or familial hierarchy, often leading to more oblique forms of refusal when the request comes from a higher-status individual.

Western perspectives focus on:

☒ **Individualism:** Western societies generally prioritise individualism, where personal choice and self-determination are highly valued. This cultural paradigm supports the idea that it's acceptable, and even expected, for individuals to refuse offers that do not align with their personal goals or boundaries.

- ☒ **Direct communication:** Western cultures tend to favour direct communication. Being clear and straightforward when declining an offer is often seen as a sign of honesty and integrity. Refusing offers by saying 'NO' is less about maintaining group harmony and more about personal authenticity and clear boundary setting.

- ☒ **Egalitarianism:** Although not uniform across all Western societies, there's a stronger inclination towards egalitarian relationships. This flattening of hierarchies supports the idea that everyone, regardless of status, has the right to refuse or accept offers based on personal choice.

The concept of saying 'NO' to build a life of choice without obligation is influenced by whether a culture values the group over the individual or vice versa. In Eastern cultures, saying 'NO' can involve navigating complex social cues and maintaining harmony, whereas in Western cultures, it often involves asserting individual rights and boundaries.

Understanding these cultural nuances is essential for international interactions and for individuals who aim to live authentically within their cultural contexts while respecting others' ways of life.

Indigenous and tribal perspectives

Many indigenous cultures have a strong sense of community and sharing. Refusals might be rare and, when necessary, are often done in a way that maintains the relationship and communal ties.

In indigenous and tribal communities, the approach to refusing offers by saying 'NO' and the concept of choice without obligation are deeply intertwined with cultural values, social structures and a communal way of life.

Here's a closer look at how these influence thought processes within these communities:

- ☒ Heavily ingrained is communal decision-making, which influences indigenous and tribal societies and often operates on a consensus-based decision-making process that emphasises the wellbeing of the community as a whole. In such contexts, saying 'NO' is not just a personal choice but a communal consideration. Choices are made with group consensus in mind, and obligations are communal rather than individual.

- ☒ Interconnectedness and reciprocity impact many indigenous cultures. Refusing an offer often goes beyond personal preference and is considered within the context of reciprocity and the ongoing relationships between individuals and the broader community or ecosystem.

- ☒ Indigenous and tribal communities hold elders and traditional ways of life in high regard. Refusing offers by saying 'NO' to an elder or a community decision can be complex and may require a sensitive approach that respects cultural norms and hierarchies.

- ☒ The indigenous holistic view of the world considers the spiritual, physical, emotional and mental dimensions of life. Decisions, including refusals, are made considering the impact on all these aspects, not just individual desire or gain.

- ☒ Indigenous communities may use non-verbal cues or more subtle forms of communication to indicate refusal. This can help maintain harmony and respect within tightly knit communities, where confrontation is avoided.

- ☒ Choices are often made with long-term sustainability in mind, including the sustainability of relationships. Saying 'NO' may be influenced by considerations of what is sustainable for the community and future generations, rather than what satisfies immediate personal desires.

In essence, saying 'NO' within indigenous and tribal communities is a complex act that involves balancing personal autonomy with communal responsibility, long-term sustainability, and a deep respect for tradition and the interconnectedness of life. These considerations shape a communal way of thinking that values the collective over the individual, and decisions are often made with the impact on the community and environment as a priority.

Spiritual and religious perspectives

In some spiritual and religious contexts – such as within certain Christian, Jewish and Islamic teachings – saying 'NO' to certain offers might be encouraged if the offer goes against one's faith or moral code. Here's how these principles influence thought and action across different beliefs:

- ☒ **Hinduism (Bhagavad Gita, Vedas, Upanishads, Puranas):** Encourages individuals to follow their dharma (duty/ righteous path) while making choices that align with their karma (action and its consequences). Saying 'NO' is part of exercising personal dharma and making choices that lead to spiritual growth and liberation (moksha).

- ☒ **Buddhism (Tripitaka):** Emphasises the Middle Way and the path to enlightenment, which involves making choices that reduce suffering. Refusing actions that cause harm or attachment is essential to following the Noble Eightfold Path, showcasing the importance of discernment and personal agency in spiritual development.

- ☒ **Taoism (Tao Te Ching):** Advocates for living in harmony with the Tao (the Way) and emphasises simplicity, spontaneity and non-action (Wu Wei) when appropriate. Saying 'NO' aligns with the principle of non-action when actions do not accord with the natural way of things.

- ☒ **Confucianism (Analects of Confucius):** Stresses the importance of societal roles, ethics and moral rectitude. Saying 'NO' can be seen as a way to maintain moral integrity and fulfil one's duties correctly within the structure of family and society.

- ☒ **Sikhism (Guru Granth Sahib):** Highlights the importance of living a life of truth, compassion and community service. Refusal of an offer by saying 'NO' in this context means rejecting actions that divert from the path of God or fulfilling one's obligations towards the community and God.

- ☒ **Judaism (Tanakh, Talmud):** Focuses on following God's Ten Commandments and the moral and ethical guidelines outlined in the Torah. Saying 'NO' is essential when it comes to resisting actions that violate these commandments and ethical teachings.

- ☒ **Zoroastrianism (Avesta):** Centres on the cosmic struggle between truth and falsehood. Making choices, including refusals, based on truth and righteousness is crucial for supporting the order of good and combating evil.

- ☒ **Islam (The Quran):** The Quran, the holy book of Islam, emphasises principles such as autonomy, personal responsibility and the moral implications of choices, though it does not explicitly discuss the concept of saying 'NO' in the context of building a life of choice without obligation. Instead, it offers guidance on the importance of making decisions that are in harmony with one's ethical and spiritual obligations, the wellbeing of the community, and the laws of God. These principles encourage Muslims to make deliberate choices that are in alignment with their faith, personal wellbeing, and communal harmony.

In all of these traditions, saying 'NO' reflects a deeper engagement with one's beliefs, values and the ethical frameworks provided by these religious and philosophical texts. It involves a conscious decision-making process that respects personal autonomy, ethical integrity and often the wellbeing of the community.

Across these diverse teachings, the act of refusal is tied to larger concepts of duty, morality, spiritual growth and harmony, emphasising its significance in leading a fulfilling and righteous life. These texts are integral to the religious and philosophical traditions they belong to and form the basis for the moral, ethical and spiritual lives of their followers.

Historic examples of saying 'NO'

Let me offer some examples of significant 'NO' answers from the past century, each with its own weight and impact:

- ☒ **Mahatma Gandhi's nonviolent resistance to British rule in India.** His 'NO' to colonial oppression ultimately led to India's independence and inspired countless movements for civil rights and self-determination.

- ☒ **Rosa Parks refusing to give up her seat on a bus in Montgomery, Alabama.** Rosa sparked the Montgomery Bus Boycott and a pivotal moment in the American Civil Rights Movement.

- ☒ **Nelson Mandela's refusal to compromise on apartheid in South Africa.** His 'NO' to racial segregation helped dismantle a brutal system and paved the way for a more democratic nation.

- ☒ **Winston Churchill's 'no surrender' speech during World War II.** This defiant stance galvanised British resistance and played a crucial role in defeating Nazi Germany.

- ☒ **The women's suffragette movement's continuous 'NO' to disenfranchisement.** Their unwavering demand for voting rights ultimately led to women's suffrage in many countries.

- ☒ **The Stonewall Riots.** The collective 'NO' to police harassment and discrimination against LGBTIQA+ individuals ignited a movement for LGBTIQA+ rights and equality.

- ☒ **Resistance from First Nations People to mining and resource extraction on their lands.** Their ongoing 'NO' protects ecosystems and cultural heritage while demanding respect for ancestral rights.

- ☒ **Jackie Robinson's courage and refusal to accept racial discrimination, both in the military and his career.** Robinson helped break the colour barrier in Major League Baseball. His actions paved the way for countless Black athletes in various sports.

- ☒ **Kathrine Switzer's entry into the Boston Marathon in 1967.** Her defiance of the ban on women runners opened doors for female participation in long-distance running and beyond.

- ☒ **Netflix chooses to keep *Cuties*.** Netflix faced backlash and calls for subscription cancellations over the release of the French film *Cuties*, criticised for its portrayal of young girls. Netflix decided to continue streaming the film, supporting the filmmaker's right to freedom of expression and the film's intended critique of societal pressures on young girls. This decision highlighted Netflix's commitment to creative freedom, despite potential short-term subscriber losses.

- ☒ **Yahoo! turns down Microsoft.** In 2008, Yahoo! rejected a $44.6 billion buyout offer from Microsoft. While this decision was heavily criticised at the time – especially as Yahoo!'s value declined in the following years – it was based on the belief that Yahoo! could achieve greater value independently. The decision exemplifies how businesses sometimes say 'NO' to enormous offers, betting on their own path forward despite immense pressure.

- ☒ **Apple refuses to modify software for the FBI.** In 2016, Apple was asked by the FBI to unlock an iPhone used by a suspect in a terrorism case. Apple refused to create a backdoor to their software, citing privacy concerns for all users. Although this decision led to a legal battle and public scrutiny, it solidified Apple's reputation for protecting user privacy, which was important to its customer base.

Modern society's emphasis on assertiveness

The emphasis on assertiveness in modern society undeniably impacts how individuals act and communicate refusals or rejections by saying 'NO'. This transformation has led to nuanced perspectives and arguments regarding the role and perception of assertiveness, especially in the context of saying 'NO'.

In this section we explore some diverse viewpoints.

Positive outcomes of increased assertiveness:

- ☒ **Empowerment and autonomy:** Assertiveness is seen as a means of empowerment, enabling individuals to express their needs and desires without aggression or passivity. It supports personal autonomy and decision-making, allowing people to say 'NO' with confidence.

- ☒ **Clear communication:** Advocates argue that assertiveness leads to clearer communication, reducing misunderstandings and fostering honest relationships. Being assertive in refusal is seen as a way to set transparent boundaries and expectations.

- ☒ **Professional growth:** In the workplace, assertiveness is often linked to leadership qualities and professional growth. Assertive communication, including the ability to refuse respectfully and firmly, is valued as a skill that contributes to effective management and team dynamics.

- ☒ **Mental health and wellbeing:** Being able to assertively say 'NO' is associated with better mental health outcomes. It helps individuals avoid overcommitment, stress and burnout, promoting a healthier work–life balance.

Challenges of increased assertiveness:

- ☒ **Cultural sensitivity:** Critics note that assertiveness, especially in refusal, may not be universally appreciated or appropriate due to cultural differences. In cultures where indirect communication and group harmony are valued, assertive refusals might be perceived as rude or insensitive, particularly when status and hierarchy are involved.

- ☒ **Perceptions of selfishness:** Some argue that assertiveness, particularly the act of saying 'NO', can sometimes be misinterpreted as selfishness or lack of cooperation, potentially harming relationships.

- ☒ **Gender bias:** The perception of assertiveness can be gendered, with research suggesting that assertive behaviour from women, especially in professional settings, is often judged more harshly than similar behaviour from men.

  My wife, Suzi, the former CEO of Women & Leadership Australia, has found this to be a real obstacle for many women, particularly in male-dominated environments. It is often a topic to be addressed in her executive coaching sessions, workshops and professional speaking engagements.[3] I'm shocked that this still exists in businesses – not good enough!

  The following examples are generalisations and it's important to recognise that there are variations and

---

3   For more information on Suzi's work and her programs, visit www.suzifinkelstein.com.au

exemptions for individuals and organisational differences. These examples are from Suzi's work and substantiated by research.

- **Professional settings:**

  Men: In the workplace, assertive men are often seen as natural leaders and are more likely to be promoted and rewarded.

  Women: Assertive women may face a backlash or be perceived as difficult to work with, and can be labelled as 'bossy'. This can hinder their career progression and lead to harsher criticism and fewer opportunities for advancement.

- **Communication styles:**

  Men: Direct and assertive men are generally accepted as being strong leaders and respected for being 'strategic' in their thinking.

  Women: Women using direct and assertive communication may be viewed as aggressive and lacking interpersonal skills. They are often expected to balance assertiveness with warmth and empathy.

- **Emotional responses:**

  Men: Emotional responses to assertive men are often neutral or positive, with assertiveness seen as a sign of strength.

  Women: Assertive women may provoke resentment in others, who might perceive their behaviour as ineffective or weak.

- ☒ **Risk of misuse:** There's a concern that assertiveness can be misused or confused with aggression, leading to confrontations rather than constructive dialogue. The line between being assertive and being aggressive can sometimes be thin and subjective.

A balanced perspective of increased assertiveness:

- ☒ **Adaptability and flexibility:** A balanced view suggests the importance of being adaptable in assertiveness, tailoring one's approach to context, relationships and cultural norms.

This flexibility can help navigate the potential downsides of assertiveness.

☒ **Emotional intelligence:** Emotional intelligence plays a crucial role in assertive communication. Recognising and responding to the emotions of oneself and others can guide how and when to say 'NO' effectively.

☒ **Continual learning and growth:** Assertiveness is seen as a skill that requires ongoing development, reflection and adjustment. Learning from experiences and feedback can enhance one's ability to communicate refusals in a way that is both effective and sensitive to the situation.

Modern society's evolution of assertiveness indeed shapes how we express refusal and navigate choices. While there are compelling arguments for the benefits of assertiveness, it's clear that its application and reception can be complex and influenced by cultural, social and interpersonal dynamics. Balancing assertiveness with empathy, adaptability and emotional intelligence emerges as a nuanced approach to saying 'NO' and managing interactions in today's diverse and changing world.

Generational attitudes to 'NO'

Understanding how individuals from different generations express their thoughts and feelings, particularly when saying 'NO' to societal expectations or obligations, requires examining the historical, social and technological contexts that shaped each generation's communication styles and values.

Over the last 100 years, we've seen remarkable changes in society, technology and the way people interact with each other. Here's a broad overview of how different generations have approached this challenge.

☒ **The Greatest Generation (1901–1927):**

Context: Grew up during the Great Depression and World War II.

Expression: This generation was characterised by a strong sense of duty, sacrifice and loyalty to country and family.

Saying 'NO' to societal expectations was less common due to these values. When they did assert their paths, it was often through actions rather than words – making significant life choices that reflected their personal beliefs and priorities, sometimes at great personal cost.

☒ **The Silent Generation (1928–1945):**

Context: Came of age during post-war prosperity but under the shadow of the Cold War.

Expression: Known for their conformity and the 'organisation man' ethos, members of the Silent Generation were less likely to openly challenge societal norms. However, when they chose to forge their own paths, they did so through quiet resistance and by excelling in the spaces allowed to them, often paving the way for future change through perseverance and integrity rather than overt confrontation.

☒ **Baby Boomers (1946–1964):**

Context: Grew up during a time of great social change, including the Civil Rights Movement, the Vietnam War protests and the sexual revolution.

Expression: Boomers were vocal in their desire for change and willing to say 'NO' to traditional paths. They expressed their thoughts and feelings through protests, music, literature and public discourse. They were pioneers in challenging the status quo and advocating for a life of personal fulfilment beyond societal expectations.[4]

☒ **Generation X (1965–1980):**

Context: Came of age in the economic downturn of the 1970s and 1980s, the rise of divorce rates, and the advent of personal computing.

Expression: Gen Xers, often labelled as 'latchkey kids', grew up with scepticism of institutions and valuing independence. They expressed their autonomy and resistance to obligation through a DIY culture, alternative

---

4   I'm a proud Baby Boomer and I often enjoy challenging the status quo, and am proud to wear the pioneer T-shirt.

media and cynical humour that challenged previous generations' norms. Their approach to saying 'NO' was to prioritise work–life balance and create new ways of living that valued autonomy.

- ☒ **Millennials (1981–1996):**

    Context: Millennials grew up with the internet and rapid technological advancements, along with the impact of 9/11 and the 2007–08 financial crisis.

    Expression: This generation has been more open and expressive about their feelings and desires, using digital platforms to share their voices. They have challenged traditional paths by advocating for social issues, seeking meaningful work, and emphasising mental health and self-care. Their way of saying 'NO' has often involved public discourse, social media activism and a willingness to openly discuss and challenge societal expectations.

- ☒ **Generation Z (1997–2012):**

    Context: These true digital natives have grown up with smartphones, social media and an increasingly polarised political landscape.

    Expression: Gen Zers are digitally savvy and use social media platforms not just for self-expression but also as a tool for activism and change. They are highly aware of global issues and are vocal about demanding change, often blending humour with activism. Their approach to saying 'NO' is through digital activism, creating inclusive communities, and pushing for systemic change at an early age.

Each generation has found its unique ways to express dissent and choose personal paths over societal obligations. The methods have evolved from more subdued and action-oriented expressions to vocal, public displays of resistance and calls for change, heavily influenced by technological advancements and changing social norms.

Statistics and research suggest that saying 'NO' has significant benefits for both individuals and organisations, particularly in terms of mental health, productivity and establishing healthy boundaries.

A survey of more than 1000 Americans revealed younger generations, especially Gen Z, struggle the most with saying 'NO' and setting healthy boundaries. Nearly half (48%) of Americans surveyed confessed to attending events they wanted to skip, primarily out of guilt or obligation. This tendency was highest among Gen Z, with 66% going to unwanted events, followed by 48% of Millennials, 43% of Gen X, and only 26% of Baby Boomers.

The difficulty in saying 'NO' affects more than just social engagements; it also impacts work–life balance, personal time and mental health. Interestingly, the survey found a gender difference, with 65% of women compared to 49% of men admitting to having trouble saying 'NO'.[5]

In the workplace, saying 'NO' is crucial for managing workload and preventing burnout. With meetings increasing by almost 70% since 2020, learning to decline non-essential meetings and communicate effectively about one's capacity can help maintain productivity and work–life balance.[6] Establishing boundaries by saying 'NO' can lead to better mental health, more productive use of time and healthier personal and professional relationships. It allows individuals to prioritise their wellbeing and focus on tasks and activities that align with their goals and values.[7]

Modern society places a high value on assertiveness as a communication skill and personal trait, recognising it as essential for effective interaction and boundary setting. Assertiveness enables individuals to express their thoughts, feelings and needs directly and appropriately, which is particularly relevant when refusing an offer by saying 'NO'.

The question this raises for us all is how do we tactfully respond to these situations and requests knowing we want to maintain or enhance relationships, not destroy them. Saying 'NO' needs to be done with respect and empathy.

I can hear my late dad's voice:

---

5   https://thrivingcenterofpsych.com/blog/setting-healthy-boundaries.
6   https://reclaim.ai/blog/how-to-say-no-professionally.
7   Ibid.

Son, haven't I told
you this many times
before?

It's not what you say,
but the way you say it.

Don Finkelstein (1930–2022)

CHAPTER 2 REVIEW

In essence, the ability to say 'NO' is a powerful tool shaped by a complex interplay of culture, history, religion and personal psychology. Navigating this requires an understanding of your own boundaries, the expectations of others, and the context in which you operate. The teachings from the past and the evolution of modern society offer valuable insights into making autonomous choices that honour your values while being considerate of societal norms and relationships.

Top takeaways and lessons learned

☒ **Cultural sensitivity:** Recognise that refusal is viewed differently across cultures, and what may be appropriate in one culture could be offensive in another.

☒ **Value of tact:** Even in cultures that value directness, tact and empathy can go a long way in preserving relationships when refusing offers.

☒ **Harmony vs autonomy:** The balance between maintaining social harmony and asserting personal autonomy is a delicate one and varies widely between Eastern and Western cultures.

☒ **Historical wisdom:** History provides examples of wise individuals who understood the power of 'NO' and navigated their refusal with wisdom and respect for their culture's values.

☒ **Religious guidance:** Many religious teachings provide frameworks for when and how to refuse, often tying the act of refusal to moral and ethical standards.

☒ **Assertiveness as a skill:** Modern perspectives on assertiveness emphasise its importance as a personal and professional skill, while also acknowledging the need for balance and cultural awareness.

- ☒ **Interpersonal dynamics:** In any refusal, consider the impact on interpersonal dynamics and the potential for future interactions.

- ☒ **Self-care and boundaries:** Modern psychology supports the setting of boundaries as crucial for self-care and personal wellbeing.

- ☒ **Generational differences:** Be aware of how generational values and experiences shape approaches to refusal and the expression of personal autonomy.

PART II
LEARNING TO SAY 'NO' TO TRANSFORM YOUR OWN LIFE

Chapter 3

Defining and defending your boundaries

Understanding boundaries

Boundaries help define who we are and what we stand for – they become our definition of self. They are a crucial part of our identity and self-concept. When we have a clear sense of self, we are better equipped to recognise when something doesn't align with our values and are more likely to say 'NO'.

Protection of resources is what's needed to enable our boundaries to guard our time, energy and emotional wellbeing. Understanding our limits helps us manage these resources effectively and decline requests that would deplete them. Boundaries create a safe space for our emotions, allowing us to engage in interactions that make us feel secure and avoid those that cause us stress or discomfort. This contributes to better health and balance by preventing overcommitment and stress, which can lead to burnout and other health issues.

Understanding our boundaries is critical to the process of saying 'NO' for several interrelated psychological, emotional and practical reasons. These boundaries define the limits of what we are willing to accept and do, and they play a vital role in maintaining our integrity and wellbeing. Saying 'NO' to unwanted endeavours will help you safeguard your important resources, which include time, money, energy and reputation.

Overcommitment, stress and eventually resentment towards others or ourselves can result from failing to recognise or keep our limits, which can also affect our emotional health. Repeatedly saying 'YES' when we want to say 'NO' might cause emotional exhaustion and burnout since we are putting our mental and physical energy into things that don't suit our needs or desires.

Personal autonomy is a prerequisite for defining and defending your boundaries. We can exert control over our lives when we have boundaries. Knowing when to draw the line enables us to make decisions on our own, and ensure that our behaviours are the product of conscious decisions rather than external pressures or duties – establishing clearly defined boundaries gives us the ability to select what we engage in. Effective communication helps us convey our limits to others in a way that can avoid miscommunications and confrontations. Honest interactions mean being aware of our boundaries, which enables us to communicate openly with others.

Taking care of our mental health is very important. Guilt and worry are the results of not setting boundaries. By defending our priorities and mental space, we are not rejecting the individual. Self-respect is being mindful of our limits, a sign of respect for ourselves and others. It sends a message about the value of our time, feelings and efforts.

Sound relationships with others are built on clear boundaries. They facilitate a healthy balance of reciprocity and keep partnerships from becoming abusive or one-sided. Mutual respect is the net result of building these relationships. By setting clear limits, we show others how to treat us.

Boundaries in the workplace keep work from invading personal life, which is crucial for long-term career happiness. Professional honesty and development give us work–life balance and harmony. This aids in moulding our career path in a manner consistent with our professional objectives and values.

The energy that each of us possesses is limited. We can save this energy for genuinely meaningful relationships and exchanges. Being aware of our limits gives us the strength to resist peer pressure and make decisions that are right for us, rather than just following the influence of the group.

Our decisions are guided by our ethical and moral standards. Our limits frequently serve as a reflection of our moral compass. By adhering to them, we can make moral choices and turn down proposals that violate our moral or ethical standards. Establishing boundaries also means understanding when to say 'NO' to something that could harm someone else, like engaging in a potentially dangerous activity. Compassion is the foundation for all of this.

In essence, understanding our boundaries is not about limiting ourselves but rather about creating a framework within which we can operate with integrity, authenticity and respect – both for ourselves and for others. It allows us to navigate life's myriad choices with a clear sense of direction, enabling us to build a life that reflects our true preferences and commitments, free from unwarranted obligations.

The psychology of setting boundaries

The psychology of saying 'NO' is a complex interplay of cognitive, emotional, social and professional factors. Let's delve into each of these facets to understand how they contribute to our capacity to set boundaries and how they can be navigated to enable a life of autonomous decision-making.

Cognitive processing

Cognitive processing plays a pivotal role in the psychology of setting boundaries as it involves the mental functions related to perception, memory, judgement and decision-making. Here's how different aspects of cognitive processing contribute to the ability to say 'NO':

- ☒ **Perception and interpretation:** When faced with a request or demand, our brains first perceive the information and interpret its significance. This involves the sensory cortices

Living with intention means saying no to the things that aren't important so we can say yes to what matters most.

Crystal Paine

and the association areas of the brain, which process the sensory data and contextual cues. How we interpret a request – whether as a demand, an opportunity or a threat – can influence our willingness to say 'NO'.

- ☒ **Our attentional systems within our brains:** These are responsible for our attention and focus, including the reticular activating system and parts of the prefrontal cortex, which determine what information we focus on. If we're attuned to the potential negative outcomes of saying 'YES' (such as stress or overcommitment), we're more likely to say 'NO'.

- ☒ **The cognitive processes:** These are involved in saying 'NO' and are dynamic and interconnected. They require us to perceive, focus, remember, predict, resolve conflict, exert control, reason ethically, consider social factors and communicate. Enhancing our cognitive skills in these areas can lead to a more robust ability to say 'NO' when it serves our best interests.

- ☒ **Our decision-making framework:** This is the cognitive processing capability that's central to decision-making. Saying 'NO' involves engaging with this framework, where we evaluate the request against our current priorities and resources, and the potential consequences of acceptance or refusal. Cognitive biases such as the sunk cost fallacy,[8] where we continue a behaviour as a result of previously invested resources, can hinder our ability to say 'NO'.

- ☒ **Predictive analysis:** This comes into play because we're wired to predict outcomes based on past experiences. If past refusals led to negative outcomes, we might be conditioned to avoid saying 'NO' to prevent expected negative consequences.

- ☒ **Mental scripts:** We operate according to mental scripts formed by our upbringing and experiences. If our script

---

8   The sunk cost fallacy is a cognitive bias in which individuals continue investing in a decision or project based on the cumulative prior investment (time, money, effort) rather than current or future benefits. This often leads to irrational decision-making, as people are unwilling to abandon a failing course of action due to the resources already committed.

says that saying 'NO' is associated with being rude or unkind, we may struggle to refuse requests even when necessary for our wellbeing.

Emotional regulation

Emotional regulation is a critical component of the psychology of setting boundaries.

Emotional regulation is about managing our internal emotional landscape to make decisions that are in our best interest. It involves a balance of understanding and controlling our emotions, which is necessary to assert ourselves and say 'NO' when it aligns with our personal boundaries and values.

Here's how emotional regulation plays a role in the ability to set boundaries:

☒ **Guilt and obligation:** Emotionally, guilt often serves as a barrier to saying 'NO'. We may feel an internalised sense of obligation, a worry about letting others down, or a fear of being perceived negatively. Managing these emotions is key to asserting our choices without falling prey to unnecessary guilt.

☒ **Stress response:** Refusal can trigger a stress response, particularly if we're conflict-averse. The anticipation of a negative reaction can lead to anxiety, which we might avoid by acquiescing rather than facing the discomfort of saying 'NO'.

☒ **Assertiveness and self-worth:** Emotional regulation also ties into our self-esteem. When we feel worthy and have a solid sense of self-worth, we're more likely to be assertive and set healthy boundaries.

Social dynamics

Social dynamics play a crucial role in the psychology of setting boundaries. As social creatures, our interactions with others are not mere exchanges but are embedded in a complex web of social norms, expectations and relationships that deeply affect our behaviour and decision-making processes.

Here's how social dynamics play a role in the ability to set boundaries.

Influence of social norms and expectations:

- ☒ **Conformity:** Social norms often dictate appropriate behaviours and responses in various situations. The pressure to conform can lead individuals to comply with requests even when they would prefer not to, for fear of social sanctions or being perceived as an outcast.

- ☒ **Social conditioning:** From an early age, individuals are conditioned to behave in socially acceptable ways. This often includes being cooperative and accommodating, which can make the act of saying 'NO' feel like a breach of social etiquette or a sign of noncooperation.

The role of relationships:

- ☒ **Interpersonal dependencies:** Human relationships are characterised by a degree of interdependence. Saying 'NO' might threaten the give-and-take balance, potentially leading to guilt or anxiety about harming the relationship.

- ☒ **Social hierarchies:** In any group or society there are hierarchies, and those with less perceived power may find it particularly difficult to refuse requests from 'superiors' due to fears of repercussions or a desire to curry favour.

Group membership and identity:

- ☒ **Group cohesion:** The desire to maintain harmony within a group can make it difficult to say 'NO', especially if the group values cohesion and unity over individual expression.

- ☒ **Identity and belonging:** People often define their identities within the context of their group memberships. Saying 'NO' can sometimes feel like a rejection of the group, risking one's sense of belonging and identity within that group.

Social learning:

- ☒ **Modelling behaviour:** You learn social behaviours from observing others. If key figures in your life rarely assert their boundaries, you might learn to emulate this lack of assertion.

☒ **Reinforcement:** If saying 'YES' has historically been met with positive reinforcement (such as praise or acceptance), while saying 'NO' has led to negative consequences, these outcomes can strongly influence future behaviours.

Communication and expression:

☒ **Language and culture:** How refusal is communicated varies greatly across cultures, and in some, direct refusal is frowned upon, leading to more indirect forms of communication that can complicate the act of saying 'NO'.

☒ **Assertive communication:** The ability to communicate one's refusal assertively, clearly, and respectfully is a skill that can be influenced by social dynamics. Those who are not encouraged or taught to be assertive may find it difficult to express refusal.

Sociocultural factors:

☒ **Cultural values:** Different cultures have varying expectations about assertiveness, independence and individualism, which can influence how comfortable individuals feel about saying 'NO'.

☒ **Gender roles:** Traditional gender roles can impact the ability to refuse, with women often being socialised to be more accommodating and nurturing, potentially making it harder to assert boundaries.

Impact on self-concept:

☒ **Social reflection:** How others respond to our refusals can reflect back on our self-concept. Repeated negative responses can erode confidence and assertiveness, while positive responses can reinforce them.

☒ **Role in social structure:** Individuals often play multiple roles (parent, employee, friend), and each role comes with its own set of expectations regarding the ability to say 'NO'. Navigating them can be complex and context dependent.

Overall, the ability to say 'NO' is not merely a personal choice but is heavily influenced by the social context in which one operates. Understanding and navigating these social dynamics is crucial for individuals to assert their boundaries effectively and maintain a sense of autonomy within their social worlds. To do this, individuals must often balance their own needs and values with the expectations and needs of the groups to which they belong.

Professional repercussions

In the workplace, the stakes of defining and defending your boundaries can feel particularly high due to the potential impact on one's career and livelihood.

Career progression:

☒ Employees may fear that saying 'NO' to additional work, projects or overtime will be viewed as a lack of commitment or ambition, potentially affecting promotions or career advancement.

☒ There's a concern that turning down opportunities, even if they're not aligned with one's career goals, might result in being passed over for future prospects.

Professional relationships:

☒ Maintaining positive relationships with superiors, colleagues and subordinates is crucial in a professional setting. Saying 'NO' can be fraught with anxiety about damaging these relationships and the potential for a hostile work environment.

☒ The professional network is critical for career success. Individuals may fear that saying 'NO' could lead to being excluded from important networks or professional circles.

Performance evaluation:

☒ Many worry that refusal to take on additional tasks or projects could lead to negative evaluations, impacting bonuses, raises or job security.

- ☒ In performance-driven cultures, saying 'YES' is often rewarded; the implication is that saying 'NO' will have the opposite effect.

Leadership perception:

- ☒ For those in or aspiring to leadership positions, there's a delicate balance between being seen as a team player and setting boundaries. Leaders may feel pressured to model a 'can-do' attitude at all times.

- ☒ There may be a misconception that leaders should be omnipotent and handle all challenges without refusal, which can lead to unsustainable workloads and stress.

Overcoming fears

The fear of jeopardising social ties and professional repercussions requires a nuanced approach, balancing the desire to maintain relationships and progress with the need for personal wellbeing and career satisfaction. By developing strategies to address these fears, individuals can learn to set boundaries in a way that preserves their relationships and supports their long-term career and personal goals.

My suggestions and tips for overcoming these fears are to:

- ☒ **Contextual decision-making:** It's essential to assess each situation on its own merits and consider the actual likelihood and impact of negative outcomes versus the perceived fear of them.

- ☒ **Clear communication:** When saying 'NO', communicate your reasoning clearly and professionally. It can help to offer alternative solutions or compromises.

- ☒ **Boundary setting:** Establishing and maintaining clear boundaries can help manage stress.

- ☒ **Self-advocacy:** Advocate for yourself and your career goals. Saying 'NO' to misaligned tasks can free up time and energy for opportunities that better serve your career objectives.

- ☒ **Building resilience:** Developing resilience can help manage the stress associated with saying 'NO'. This includes building a supportive professional network that respects boundaries.

- ☒ **Reflecting on values and goals:** Regular reflection on personal values and career goals can reinforce the importance of making decisions aligned with them, even if it means saying 'NO'.

Acknowledging and respecting your own boundaries

Acknowledging and respecting your boundaries is a fundamental step in learning to say 'NO' and crafting a life defined by personal choice rather than obligation.

The first step in acknowledging your boundaries is self-reflection. Spend time alone to consider what truly matters to you, what you value and where your limits lie. Reflect on past experiences when you felt uncomfortable or resentful – these emotions often signal that a boundary has been crossed. Through self-reflection, you can begin to identify the lines you do not wish others to cross.

Once you have reflected on your boundaries, define them clearly to yourself. Write them down if necessary. Whether it's saying 'NO' to working late, declining social invitations when you need time alone, or refusing to engage in gossip, be clear about what you are willing to accept and what you are not. The next step is to communicate your boundaries to others. This does not have to be confrontational; it can be done calmly and respectfully. It's important to articulate your limits clearly and confidently so that others understand and respect them.

Practise saying 'NO' over and over again, as it may feel foreign and just not right for some. For many, saying 'NO' can be difficult. Practise saying 'NO' in low-stakes situations to build your confidence. You can rehearse or role-play with a friend or even in front of a mirror. The more you practise, the more natural it will feel to assert your boundaries when it counts.

Be prepared to defend your boundaries.

Start small if saying 'NO' is challenging for you. Start with small refusals and work your way up to bigger ones. Turning down a minor request will give you the courage to decline more significant demands on your time and energy.

Be assertive when communicating your boundaries: use 'I' statements to express your needs and feelings without blaming or criticising others. For example, say, 'I feel over-whelmed when I take on extra projects', instead of, 'You always dump extra work on me'.

If you feel guilty about saying 'NO', offer an alternative. For instance, if you can't commit to a project, suggest a time when you might be available, or recommend someone else who could help.

It's not enough to set boundaries once; you need to reinforce them consistently. If someone continues to push against a boundary, remind them of it firmly and respectfully. Consistency is key to ensuring that your boundaries are respected. It's not easy for some to hear 'NO', so be prepared for pushback. Not everyone will respond positively when you assert your boundaries. Be prepared for some resistance, but remain firm. Remember that your boundaries are about protecting your wellbeing, not about pleasing others.

Boundaries are healthy. Many people fear that setting boundaries is selfish. It's essential to understand that healthy boundaries are a sign of self-respect and are beneficial for all parties involved. They prevent resentment and misunderstand-ings in relationships.

Respecting your limits and putting your needs first by establishing your priorities go hand in hand. It's difficult, particularly if you're accustomed to putting other people before yourself, but it's necessary for your wellbeing. Make sure you're taking care of yourself, because you deserve the same attention and care as everybody else.

Seek support from others if you find it challenging to acknowledge and respect your boundaries. Talk to friends, family or a counsellor who can provide perspective and reinforce the importance of your limits.

Learning to be comfortable with discomfort can make saying 'NO' easier. Saying 'NO' can be rather uncomfortable for some, but it's a discomfort you can learn to tolerate. The more you practise, the more comfortable you will become with the discomfort that can come with asserting yourself.

Trust your instincts

Often, your gut feelings are a good indicator of when a boundary is being tested. Trust your instincts and use them as a guide to recognise when you need to assert a boundary.

An article written by Abigail Fagan, published in *Psychology Today* (19 June 2023), emphasised 'the empowerment and liberation that can come from confidently saying no', which can help individuals set clear boundaries in their relationships, contributing to self-care, self-esteem and confidence. It suggests finding a natural and authentic way to say 'NO' – such as the 'sandwich' method, where a negative is sandwiched between two positives – can make the process easier. This method not only preserves relationships but also respects the individual's needs and priorities. Reflecting on the reasons behind a 'NO' can aid in making decisions that align with one's goals and wellbeing, indicating that saying 'NO' can be a form of self-care that creates space for activities that are more aligned with personal values and energy levels.

'NO' as a powerful boundary setter

Since it establishes boundaries for our willingness, ability and engagement in both our personal and professional lives, saying 'NO' is a powerful boundary setter. It acts as a verbal boundary, outlining precisely what we will not tolerate, accept or participate in. To preserve our sense of self and make sure that our priorities are upheld, we must engage in this act of articulation. Fundamentally, being able to say 'NO' is a sign of respect and self-preservation. Communicating our boundaries and expectations to others protects our physical, mental and emotional wellbeing.

Saying 'NO' to a new project when you're already over-whelmed at work, for example, helps you avoid overcommitting, stress and burnout while preserving your productivity and

Make sure you're taking care of yourself, because you deserve the same attention and care as everybody else.

Darren Finkelstein

calibre of work on ongoing obligations. In interpersonal interactions, this could involve turning down social invitations when you need time to yourself to safeguard your wellbeing and make sure that your social interactions are pleasurable and satisfying rather than required and taxing.

Saying 'NO' is also an essential part of relationship development and successful communication. It encourages openness and truthfulness in communication, paving the way for happier, more respected relationships. It lessens the possibility of miscommunications and animosity by establishing limits and fostering an environment where respect and understanding for one another can grow. Any relationship benefits from a dynamic that is enhanced when people feel free to express their limits and feel comfortable doing so.

Saying 'NO' strengthens our sense of autonomy and integrity by enabling us to take charge of our lives and decisions. It is a declaration of our freedom and liberation, giving us all the wonderful ability to choose, without giving in to pressure or expectations from outside sources. Saying 'NO' as a boundary setter is, in essence, a significant exercise in establishing and declaring our identity, priorities and limits. It's not just about refusing. It involves making deliberate decisions that safeguard our wellbeing and are consistent with our true selves. By establishing limits and learning to say 'NO', we can live intentionally and purposefully, achieving balance and fulfilment in the process.

Remember that asserting boundaries is a form of self-care. It's about taking control of your life and making decisions that serve your wellbeing. When you respect your boundaries, you send a message that you value yourself, which can lead to a more fulfilling life. You can begin to respect your own boundaries and say 'NO' when necessary, paving the way for a life of personal choice, free from the weight of obligation.

Top takeaways and lessons learned

☒ **Personal boundaries:** Personal boundaries are essential for preserving self-identity, emotional wellbeing, autonomy, effective communication, mental health, relationship dynamics, professional integrity, social wellbeing and upholding moral and ethical standards.

☒ **Self-identity preservation:** Knowing your boundaries helps maintain your integrity and live according to your principles. Clear boundaries prevent stress and resentment by avoiding overcommitment.

☒ **Exercising autonomy:** Boundaries enable you to make decisions that reflect your true choices, not just acquiesce to outside demands.

☒ **Clear communication:** Understanding your boundaries allows for clearer communication, reducing the potential for misunderstandings.

☒ **Foundation for healthy relationships:** Boundaries allow for balanced relationships and teach others how to interact with you respectfully.

☒ **Professional growth:** Setting work boundaries can lead to better job satisfaction and career development aligned with your goals.

☒ **Conservation of social energy:** Recognising social boundaries helps to invest time and energy in meaningful relationships and activities.

- ☒ **Resistance to peer pressure:** Firm boundaries empower you to withstand pressure and make choices that align with your best interests.

- ☒ **Expect and accept resistance:** Not everyone will understand or respect your boundaries; be prepared to reassert them calmly.

- ☒ **Self-care is paramount:** Setting boundaries is a form of self-care; it is not selfish to prioritise your wellbeing.

- ☒ **Seek support when needed:** Don't hesitate to reach out for support in maintaining your boundaries.

Chapter 4

Saying 'NO' in personal relationships

Saying 'NO' can be transformative

In personal relationships, the act of saying 'NO' can be transformative, allowing individuals to establish and maintain healthy boundaries. This is a crucial aspect explored in this book. By saying 'NO', individuals protect their time, energy and emotional wellbeing, ensuring that they are not overextended or taken advantage of by others. This doesn't mean rejecting loved ones, but rather prioritising self-care and mutual respect in relationships.

Saying 'NO' can often be challenging due to feelings of guilt or the fear of conflict. However, it is essential to understand that a well-placed 'NO' can prevent resentment and burnout. When you say 'NO' to requests or behaviours that overstep your boundaries, you create space for more meaningful and authentic connections. This act of self-respect encourages others to respect your limits, fostering a relationship dynamic where both parties feel valued and understood.

Intentional living is the art of making our own choices before others' choices make us.

Richie Norton

In the context of intimate relationships, the ability to say 'NO' is a declaration of autonomy and mutual respect. It allows partners to communicate their needs and desires honestly, leading to deeper trust and intimacy. In friendships, saying 'NO' ensures that the relationship remains balanced and reciprocal. It prevents one-sided dynamics where one person's needs consistently overshadow the other's.

Saying 'NO' in personal relationships is crucial for building a life of choice without obligation due to several reasons:

☒ Personal boundaries defined by the ability to say 'NO' help maintain one's identity.

☒ Consistently agreeing to things that don't align with one's beliefs or desires can lead to losing a sense of self.

☒ Emotional health and wellbeing can be affected by not being able to refuse; therefore, being unable to say 'NO' can result in stress, resentment and emotional exhaustion.

The ability to say 'NO' is a cornerstone of personal autonomy and empowerment. It empowers individuals to make choices based on their desires and needs rather than feeling pressured by others. Agreeing to things unwillingly can breed resentment towards the people one cares about. Saying 'NO' prevents such negative feelings from undermining relationships.

There's much to be gained through authentic relationships. When individuals can say 'NO', they are more likely to engage in activities and relationships that are genuine and fulfilling, rather than ones they feel obligated to maintain.

Role modelling and demonstrating the ability to set boundaries and say 'NO' serve as a positive example for others to follow, particularly children. Saying 'NO' helps manage the expectations of others, making it clear what one is and isn't willing to do, which is essential for a balanced relationship.

Favour quality over quantity by being selective about commitments and saying 'NO' when necessary, which ensures that one's energy is spent on high-quality interactions and relationships. Saying 'NO' prevents overcommitting oneself, which can lead to underperformance, potentially damaging relationships and personal reputation.

Supporting and encouraging reciprocity by doing unto others as we'd like done to ourselves is essential in any healthy relationship. If one party is always saying 'YES', it can create an unhealthy dynamic. Saying 'NO' helps maintain balance.

Living intentionally gives you the ability to simply say 'NO', ensuring that actions and engagements are chosen deliberately, not out of compulsion.

Finding a balance between empathy and assertiveness

Finding a balance between empathy and assertiveness (not aggression, which is typically viewed as a negative, hostile or destructive form of interaction) is crucial for saying 'NO' effectively in personal relationships.

Understanding your own needs is a foundational step in cultivating healthy personal relationships and establishing the groundwork for a life of choice rather than obligation. It entails a deep and honest self-assessment of what truly matters to you, recognising your limits, and identifying what brings you fulfilment and what causes you stress or discomfort. This self-awareness allows you to discern which requests align with your core values and life goals, and which ones may lead to overextension or resentment. Knowing your own needs isn't a static process; it's an ongoing journey of self-discovery that may evolve with time and experience. It's about tuning in to your emotions and reactions in various situations to better understand what you can happily accommodate, what you need to advocate for, and what you need to refuse to maintain your wellbeing and integrity.

Once you have a clear grasp of your personal needs, you can communicate them more effectively to others, setting the stage for assertive and empathetic interactions. It's not just about saying 'NO', but about articulating why certain things are not right for you and doing so with conviction and clarity. This clarity doesn't come overnight – it requires reflection, sometimes trial and error, and a willingness to honour your feelings. By understanding and honouring your needs, you create a filter through which decisions can be made, ensuring that your actions are congruent with your inner truth.

As you become more adept at recognising and understanding your needs, saying 'NO' becomes a proactive stance to protect your energy, time and emotional wellbeing, paving the way for a more authentic and satisfying life.

Practising assertive communication is pivotal when it comes to saying 'NO', and is an essential component for building a life of choice without falling into the traps of obligation. Assertiveness is the balanced middle ground between passivity (not standing up for oneself) and aggression (disregarding the needs and feelings of others). It involves expressing your thoughts, feelings and needs openly and honestly while respecting those of others. This form of communication is particularly relevant when refusing requests or setting boundaries, as it allows you to articulate your 'NO' clearly and confidently without causing unnecessary harm to the relationship. By being assertive, you take ownership of your decisions and communicate them in a way that is direct and respectful, thus minimising misunderstandings and potential conflicts.

Assertive communication empowers you to maintain control over your life choices. It requires you to be self-aware and to understand the reasons behind your 'NO', which in turn makes it easier to convey your stance to others. When you communicate assertively, you're not just rejecting a request; you're providing insight into your personal principles and priorities. This transparency helps others understand your perspective and can foster mutual respect, even in the face of refusal. It's a skill that, when practised regularly, enhances your ability to navigate a myriad of social interactions in a way that aligns with your authentic self.

Cultivating empathy is a crucial aspect of the process of saying 'NO', as it allows us to recognise and consider the feelings and perspectives of others while maintaining our personal boundaries. When we approach situations with empathy and compassion, we are able to understand the potential disappointment or inconvenience our refusal might cause, which can guide us in delivering our message with kindness and consideration. This doesn't mean we negate our own needs;

rather, we acknowledge the other person's request and respond with respect. Empathy in the context of refusal is about finding a compassionate way to communicate a boundary, ensuring that the other person feels heard and valued, even if their request cannot be accommodated. This can soften the impact of the refusal and maintain the integrity of the relationship.

Empathy enriches our interactions by fostering deeper connections and mutual understanding. When saying 'NO', doing so empathetically can help others see that our decisions are not arbitrary or selfish but are made with thoughtful consideration for all parties involved. It demonstrates that we are not rejecting the person but rather making a choice that is necessary for our wellbeing or circumstances. Empathy allows us to articulate our refusal in a way that can actually strengthen the relationship, as it shows we've taken the time to consider the other person's standpoint. By cultivating empathy, we ensure that our 'NO' is not just a barrier but a bridge to deeper understanding and respect between ourselves and others.

By maintaining a balance between empathy and assertiveness, you can say 'NO' in a way that respects both your needs and those of others, helping you to build a life based on choice rather than obligation.

I should have said 'NO'

I married at the ripe old age of 23, and I am still proudly married today to my first (and only) wife, Suzi, for 39 years now and still going strong. Back at the age of 27, our first child, Jeremy, was born, and two years later, in 1992, we welcomed Adam into the world.

It was a pretty big year in business for me too, as I founded a leading-edge, market-disrupting computer accessory business called Computer Office Supplies. Instead of just selling all that stationery stuff – pens, pencils, typewriter ribbon and carbon paper – we sold only the high-tech consumable products for computer rooms, big IT departments and small businesses who were brave enough to implement personal computers and data processing into their business. We were truly ahead of our time.

When saying 'NO', doing so empathetically can help others see that our decisions are not arbitrary or selfish but are made with thoughtful consideration for all parties involved.

Darren Finkelstein

We sold products like floppy disks, A3 continuous paper, magnetic tapes for mainframe computers, dot-matrix printer ink and acoustic covers (those beautifully designed wooden boxes that would sit over a printer to reduce ambient noise). They were nothing like the silent inkjet and laser printers of today. Most items we sold were high-volume consumables such as computer paper, meaning once finished they need to be regularly replaced.

Our average order value back then was around $120 and annual turnover was about $500,000, which means we processed over 4000 orders a year, or 76.9 orders per week.

The Australian Treasurer at the time was Paul Keating, and he famously described the 1990s recession as 'the recession we had to have'. Later he challenged Bob Hawke for the leadership of the Labor Party in 1991 and became Prime Minister of Australia.

The recession was simply horrible. From the mid-1980s the Australian economy was like a bubble swelling in size, which eventually burst – with immense power and much debris. Interest rates were at crippling levels of between 19% and 24%. And sadly, I was a borrower paying 22% with ANZ Bank. With that sort of overhead, one could say that I worked for the ANZ!

Can you imagine how this enormous cost of funds affected businesses of all kinds? When I look back, my business model was flawed right from the beginning, because my customers liked to buy from Computer Office Supplies due to my excellent quality of goods at very competitive prices. 'Get more quality and pay less.' I loved this ...

The foundation of my service was first-rate delivery, which frequently went above and beyond the clients' expectations with overnight and even same-day deliveries, Australia-wide. An invoice was provided to the client when the products were delivered, and their accounts payable department would occasionally take weeks – or even months – to pay.

Because I valued my suppliers and appreciated the high-quality products and prompt delivery, I made sure to pay their accounts on time, which was usually in 30 days. With my low prices, I saw this as my competitive advantage.

Happy days – or so I thought.

I was oblivious to the signs that warned of danger, danger, and more danger than I could have possibly imagined. I was so focused on SELLING, SELLING, SELLING that I was completely blind to the high expense of running the business, specifically the huge 'cost of money'. Therefore, the problem got worse the more I sold.

Regretfully, though, it took my clients an average of 120 days to pay me, so I ended up becoming their lender as well. However, I didn't impose any interest on them for any unpaid balances. Jeez, I'm such a lovely man now that I work for the bank. To put it simply, I became the clients' lender too because I paid my suppliers in full well in advance of when my clients paid me, which was around 90 days earlier.

Underpin all of this with the simple fact that the 22% interest rate on my borrowings – which funded the 90-day differential – meant my interest bill was suffocating my business.

There lies a wonderful and not-so-complicated lesson of Business 101.

It's true that the numbers never lie …

Clearly and upon reflection, what I did not control was my finances and my clients' payment terms. The number of growing debtors plus their outstanding invoice due dates should have been the first signs that trouble was brewing.

I, as the business owner, can say that I stuck my head in the sand when it came to my financials, largely because I didn't fully understand them if I am honest. My business was being suffocated by debt, my inadequate understanding of the economy at that time, and the direct correlation between my growing overdraft plus massive interest bill caused by tiny profit margins on the sale of goods and slow payments. I attempted to competitively grow the business by selling more and more products.

Everything that was going on at the time seemed like a recipe for disaster for me, being pretty young, poorly educated and inexperienced in operating a business, which meant I was commercially naïve. As you'd expect, Suzi and I faced bank-appointed administration and receivership. It was Christmas Eve that year when I laid off my entire team of 10 people and closed the doors.

My first business failed because I said 'YES'
when I should have said 'NO'.

It was a horrible Christmas.

We walked away with nothing but a massive debt of $500,000. Suzi and I lost our house to the ANZ Bank and we were left with just $500 in our account, after attempting to pay all of our creditors and legal costs. We lost all remaining self-belief too. It was a dark time.

So, I hear you ask, how is this all tied to saying 'NO' in personal relationships – well, here's the connection. My amazing late father-in-law, Hal, who was also a highly successful entrepreneur, served as the bank's guarantor for us to obtain the loan from ANZ in the first place. I will always be appreciative of his kindness and his generosity in giving Suzi, me and the kids an incredible start in life. Upon reflection, I was simply too unskilled and totally unqualified to manage such finance, and to lead this business during a challenging economic period. My self-confidence and belief system were restored over the course of several years of therapy, and I came to the realisation that I ought to have turned down the gracious offer in the first place by saying 'NO'.

In my professional speaking engagements, I frequently share this story and largely blame my lack of accountability for the company's failure. I also discuss how I wasn't mentally prepared to answer 'YES' to doing this either, even though I thought I was. Suzi and I saying 'YES' to Hal should have been a 'NO'. But I wasn't honest with myself, and desperately wanted to follow in his footsteps and navigate those difficult roads too. I thought this was my turn to shine … I guess also I just didn't want to let him down as he was so excited with the opportunity he provided for us.

The alternative ending

So, what would have been a better outcome than my ill-fated 'YES'?

Firstly, acknowledging the generosity and trust my father-in-law showed in Suzi and me by offering such support would set a positive tone for the discussion. Expressing sincere appreciation for his belief in my potential and his willingness to invest in my future could have helped affirm the bond between us, even as I prepared to share my concerns.

If we jump forward to now, I could have used my 10-step framework 'Boundaries by Design' in chapter 8. With genuine empathy and respect, what I should have said goes something like this:

> *Suzi and I would like to thank you for your kind offer to help with financing by acting as a guarantor for the loan to start our business. However, we've been debating whether or not to launch the business right now, owing in large part to my lack of understanding and commercial acumen. We are genuinely concerned since it is a significant amount of money, and we want to proceed cautiously; there is no need to start the business right away.*
>
> *While I appreciate your belief in my ability and potential, perhaps I could research and study running a business first, to gain knowledge of the financial aspects before we launch it. Perhaps, I could spend more time with you in your business first to gain a firm grasp, so I'm not as commercially clueless as I feel I am right now.*
>
> *We may accept your kind offer later. We appreciate it and love you to bits for wanting us to get a head start like you did and for believing in me, but we are not ready now.*

Knowing Hal, he would have understood this completely, and been very supportive of our decision to say 'NO'. I reckon he'd feel pretty happy that we were so honest with him.

It's now some 30+ years later, and I often think about what *could* have been. If only I:

- ☒ took full responsibility for our financial health as the owner of the business
- ☒ found the right people to bring in expertise that I did not have
- ☒ made the necessary time to better understand how it all worked

- ☒ understood the direct correlation between our sales margins and my debtor days
- ☒ recognised what the ridiculously high 22% interest rates meant for growing the business
- ☒ understood that *not* all business is good business – our slow-paying debtors of 120 days meant the more we sold, the larger our debt grew
- ☒ had harnessed my entrepreneurial energy until I had more business acumen
- ☒ made the sales COD to support the cheap pricing.

It's really hard to say 'NO' to an opportunity, especially when it comes from a friend, family member or a loved one who means well. Saying 'NO' takes guts, vision and the capacity to articulate your logic clearly with respect and empathy.

Consenting adults

Any refusal of an offer by saying 'NO', particularly in the area of interpersonal connections, is fundamentally based on the idea of 'consenting adults'. This principle underscores the importance of mutual consent and personal autonomy, which are foundational to healthy interpersonal dynamics.

In the context of physical intimacy, the concept of 'consenting adults' is crucial. It emphasises that both parties involved in any interaction or agreement must freely give their consent without coercion. Saying 'NO' is an exercise of this consent, reflecting an individual's right to make decisions about their own involvement and boundaries. This respect for personal autonomy is a cornerstone of ethical and respectful relationships.

Moreover, the notion of consent is deeply embedded in modern societal values. It aligns with legal and ethical standards that prioritise the rights and freedoms of individuals. In many jurisdictions, the idea of consent is not only a social expectation but also a legal requirement in various aspects of life, including contracts, personal relationships and professional engagements.

In practice, the ability to refuse offers or invitations respectfully and confidently is an essential aspect of maintaining healthy interpersonal boundaries. It ensures that relationships are built on genuine willingness and mutual respect rather than obligation or pressure. This is particularly important in a society that values individual rights and the integrity of personal choices. Therefore, the act of saying 'NO' is in total alignment with societal expectations regarding the autonomy and consent of adults. It emphasises the value of respect for one another, individual autonomy, and people's freedom to make decisions about their lives and bodies, free from coercion or other forms of pressure. This fundamental idea is essential for maintaining people's dignity and freedom to conduct their lives in accordance with their personal boundaries and beliefs, as well as for creating relationships that are respectful and healthy.

Fundamentally, the idea of consenting adults highlights the significance of getting consent in all interactions, especially those that are private or intimate. The conditions for consent for me are as follows: it must be freely provided, informed, and reversible at any time. It also guarantees that all participants are completely aware of, and approve of, the amount of their engagement. For me, respecting one's boundaries is a non-negotiable element of all interactions, and this understanding affirms the freedom to say 'NO' at any moment.

Saying 'NO' to particular activities such as intimacy, engagements or advancements without fear of criticism, compulsion, pressure, retaliation and violence (both physical and verbal) is crucial to preserving one's sense of self and making sure that the foundation of a romantic relationship is mutual respect and understanding.

Does 'NO' ever mean 'YES'?

'NO' is as clear-cut and straightforward as that. 'NO' is 'NO'.

As a male, I find it unacceptable and incomprehensible that other men use the statement 'you made me do it' to pathetically defend their actions. Consent must always be provided voluntarily and freely – without being forced, manipulated or under any kind of duress, including verbal and physical.

Undermining the core values of respect, autonomy and human agency is any attempt to rationalise behaviour by assigning blame or implying that a 'NO' might be mistaken for a 'YES'. It is critical to recognise and respect each person's right to establish limits and make decisions regarding their own body and experiences. A major violation of one's integrity and personal rights, disregarding or misinterpreting a 'NO' also betrays a lack of trust and respect. A clear and unequivocal agreement between two people is what constitutes consent; it is not a murky area.

Within the framework of permission and individual limits, 'NO' does not equate to any form of 'YES'. Understanding and appreciating personal autonomy and agency are fundamentally based on this idea. In order to guarantee that both parties feel respected and heard, consent is about communication, and that requires clarity and mutual understanding. Declaring 'NO' is a concise and direct way to communicate your boundaries and choices. It conveys a personal limit that reflects a person's comfort level, preferences or readiness to take a specific action or make a certain choice.

It is crucial to have explicit consent in all situations, whether social, professional or personal. Ensuring that all parties feel heard, are participating voluntarily and fully aware of the conditions is a basic feature of ethical interactions. This clarity promotes mutual respect and trust by avoiding misunderstandings and shielding people from pressure, compulsion and undesired outcomes.

Putting forth the idea that 'NO' might ever equate to 'YES' feeds dangerous misconceptions about consent that, in the worst situations, can result in abuse. It undercuts campaigns to promote and teach open communication and consent in all partnerships. Reinforcing the idea that every individual has the right to set their own boundaries and expect them to be maintained, understanding and honouring a clear 'NO' is essential for maintaining each person's dignity, safety and autonomy.

Fundamentally, a 'NO' just means 'NO', and there's no excuses for ever mistaking that.

Respecting individual agency and permission is an essential component of communication. To create situations where everyone feels appreciated, respected and free to voice their boundaries without worrying about being misunderstood or disregarded, this principle must be widely accepted and put into practice.

Effective communication without guilt

Effective communication without guilt is essential in saying 'NO' to build a life of choice, especially when 'YES' is the expected answer. Guilt often arises when there is a disparity between the actions we take and the expectations others have of us, or even the expectations we have for ourselves based on societal norms or familial pressures. When we communicate effectively and without guilt, we can assert our personal autonomy and make choices that are in our best interest, rather than succumbing to external pressures.

When you communicate effectively – expressing your thoughts and feelings clearly and confidently – you can articulate the reasons behind your decision to decline. This clarity helps the other party understand that your 'NO' is not arbitrary or capricious, but rather a considered response based on genuine reasons. Whether those reasons are personal values, current priorities or simply the desire for a different path, effective communication conveys them in a way that is understandable and, ideally, acceptable to others.

Communicating without guilt is crucial for maintaining self-confidence when saying 'NO'. Guilt can undermine our decision-making, leading to second-guessing and regret. However, when you remove guilt from the equation, you affirm your right to make decisions for yourself. This doesn't mean being insensitive to others' feelings or needs, but rather acknowledging that your first responsibility is to yourself and your own wellbeing. By doing so, you set the stage for a life guided by your choices and convictions, not by an indebtedness to others' expectations or desires.

Guilt-free communication fosters healthier relationships. When you say 'NO' with confidence and without guilt, you

Saying 'NO' without guilt allows for a level of authenticity in your personal interactions that wouldn't be possible otherwise.

Darren Finkelstein

model healthy boundaries. This sets a precedent in your relationships, demonstrating how individuals can interact with mutual respect and understanding. It also teaches others that while their requests and needs are important, they are not automatically prioritised above your own. Over time, this can lead to more balanced and equitable interactions with family and friends, where the ability to say 'NO' is respected as part of a dynamic where everyone's agency is valued.

Saying 'NO' without guilt allows for a level of authenticity in your personal interactions that wouldn't be possible otherwise. It's an honest expression of your circumstances or feelings about a situation. This honesty can deepen connections with others, as it invites them into a space of genuine dialogue and understanding. It can also prevent resentment that might arise from agreeing to things that you don't truly want to do, which can lead to frustration.

Conducting such conversations with tact, respect and clarity mitigates feelings of guilt and disappointment, while maintaining the integrity of family relationships and building a life of choice without obligation.

CHAPTER 4 REVIEW

The notion that saying 'NO' is about making choices that align with one's values and wellbeing, ultimately leading to a more authentic and fulfilling life. This chapter delves into the transformative power of saying 'NO' within personal relationships, and emphasises the importance of setting healthy boundaries to protect one's wellbeing.

Common challenges associated with saying 'NO' include guilt or fear of conflict. A well-placed 'NO' can prevent resentment and burnout. By asserting personal boundaries, individuals can foster relationships based on mutual respect and understanding, leading to deeper trust and intimacy.

Top takeaways and lessons learned

☒ **Setting boundaries:** Saying 'NO' helps establish and maintain healthy boundaries in personal relationships, ensuring individuals do not become overextended or taken advantage of by others.

☒ **Emotional and physical health:** Manage emotional energy and prevent stress, resentment and emotional exhaustion by refusing unnecessary personal commitments.

☒ **Mutual respect:** Encourage mutual respect within relationships by defining personal limits and expecting others to do the same.

☒ **Balanced relationships:** Ensure balanced and reciprocal relationships by preventing one-sided dynamics where one person's needs overshadow the other's.

☒ **Understanding personal needs:** Conduct a deep and honest self-assessment to understand what truly matters and brings fulfilment, guiding decisions about what to refuse.

☒ **Role modelling:** Demonstrate the importance of setting boundaries and saying 'NO' as a positive example for others to follow.

☒ **Managing expectations:** Set clear expectations for others about what you are and are not willing to do.

Chapter 5

Saying 'NO' at work

Saying 'NO' in the workplace requires a sophisticated approach to communication, assertiveness and creating boundaries in work environments. It entails professionally negotiating interpersonal dynamics, controlling expectations, and placing your own goals and wellbeing first while upholding relationships and professionalism. The skill is knowing when and how to politely set limits and priorities without putting undue strain on relationships or creating unneeded conflict.

It is impossible to overestimate the significance of developing the work skill of saying 'NO' to create a life of freedom from unwanted commitment. In today's hectic and demanding work settings people frequently have a tonne of duties, obligations and expectations placed on them. When people are unable to set limits or turn down unreasonable commitments, they run the risk of feeling overburdened, eventually compromising their own happiness and wellbeing. Effectively saying 'NO' enables people to focus their time, effort and resources on things that support their values and goals, which increases success, productivity and levels of satisfaction at work.

People can build mutual respect and understanding by communicating their needs and limitations to others by effectively and politely setting boundaries. In teams and organisations, this helps to foster a culture of trust, cooperation and respect, where people feel appreciated and encouraged to express their independence and put their health first.

Having the courage and integrity to handle professional challenges is made possible by learning the skill of saying 'NO' in the workplace. It gives people the ability to take charge of their own career path and exercise agency by helping them decide which opportunities and obligations to prioritise. People can make room for development, growth and significant contributions by strategically and assertively saying 'NO', which will ultimately lead to more success and fulfilment in their professional lives.

At work, having the ability to say 'NO' when necessary is crucial to managing your workload and responsibilities. It involves using dexterity to carefully balance being aggressive and assertive. While assertiveness is about strongly establishing your limits and boundaries without undermining others, aggression can involve forcefulness or even fury. Those who are conscious of this difference are better equipped to handle the dynamics at work.

Saying 'NO' doesn't always mean rejecting work outright; rather, it means setting boundaries for expectations and workload by taking on projects that align with your skills and priorities. Co-workers must develop mutual respect and trust, and open communication can help with this. Giving concise justifications for declining an assignment or other alternatives helps foster understanding and teamwork.

Saying 'NO' in the job eventually boils down to having the confidence to stand up for yourself while maintaining professionalism and building relationships.

Finding a balance between aggression and assertiveness

To communicate successfully and maintain strong relationships in professional contexts, it is imperative to distinguish between aggression and assertiveness. The ability to respectfully and clearly express your desires and thoughts while also honouring

I don't say no because I am so busy. I say no because I don't want to be so busy.

Courtney Carver

the rights and boundaries of others is what it means to be assertive. It's standing up for yourself without going against other people's rights or acting belligerently.

Aggressive action or speech is characterised by hostility, intimidation or the use of force. As it usually involves disregarding the rights and sentiments of others, it can produce friction and conflict. Aggressive behaviours such as yelling at someone, blaming them or threatening them are instances of destructive efforts to exert control over others.

Knowing a few key strategies that allow people to respect their boundaries, be professional and maintain positive relationships while saying 'NO' in a professional situation is essential for effective time management. This self-awareness enables you to confidently evaluate requests or actions to see whether they align with your objectives and skills. It is necessary that you respond to demands you are unable to meet as soon as possible and clearly; avoid ambiguity or procrastination. By providing a brief explanation or replacement option along with a polite explanation of your decision, you can prevent resentment or misconceptions.

Offering assistance or backing to the extent that you are able, particularly when the request is not explicitly accepted, demonstrates kindness and a desire to assist the team's successes. You can create an environment at work where people respect one another and work together by consistently upholding your boundaries and priorities with dignity and respect.

Understanding the distinction between assertiveness and aggression is crucial because it influences the effectiveness of communication in the workplace. Assertive communication fosters cooperation and trust because it allows individuals to voice their thoughts honestly and confidently while also considering those of others. It promotes healthy boundaries, facilitates problem-solving and enhances collaboration. On the other hand, antagonistic communication will weaken relationships, erode trust and create a hostile work environment. It frequently leads to conflict and defensiveness, which hinders effective communication and joint efforts. By alienating clients, supervisors or co-workers, aggressive behaviour can also damage a person's reputation and prospects in the workplace.

Our ability to discriminate between assertiveness and aggression is critical for maintaining healthy work relationships. People can respectfully and firmly express their needs and boundaries while also appreciating the rights and opinions of others by employing assertive communication tactics.

Always keep in mind that there are no justifications for acts of violence, rudeness or hostility.

Agreeing to responsibilities

In the workplace, agreeing to responsibilities while maintaining the ability to say 'NO' effectively is a delicate balancing act. It involves a strategic approach that considers your own capacity and boundaries while also aligning with the goals and expectations of the team or organisation. This fosters harmony and productivity.

Have a clear understanding of your own workload and capabilities. Assessing your current commitments and priorities allows you to make informed decisions about taking on additional responsibilities. It's crucial to be realistic about what you can handle without overextending yourself. Consider factors such as deadlines, complexity and the potential impact on other projects. If a task aligns with your skills and objectives, and you can take it on without sacrificing the quality of your work or neglecting other commitments, agreeing to it may be appropriate. However, if taking on the task would stretch you too thin or compromise your ability to fulfil your existing responsibilities, it's important to assertively communicate your limitations. This involves saying 'NO' in a respectful and professional manner while also providing a brief explanation of your reasons for declining. It's helpful to offer alternatives or suggest solutions, such as delegating the task to someone else or renegotiating deadlines, to demonstrate your commitment to finding a mutually beneficial outcome.

Effective communication with your colleagues and supervisors is key to managing your work and responsibilities. By being transparent about your availability, priorities and limitations, you can build trust and collaboration within the team. This open dialogue allows for better coordination and

*Having the ability to say 'NO' when necessary is crucial
to managing your workload and responsibilities.*

allocation of tasks, also ensuring that everyone's contributions are valued and respected.

Agreeing to responsibilities in the workplace requires a thoughtful and proactive approach that balances individual needs with team objectives. By being mindful of your own limitations and communicating assertively and respectfully, you can effectively manage your workload while still building a life of choice without unnecessary obligations.

Establishing mutual respect and trust

In the workplace, building mutual respect and trust through open communication is essential, particularly when it comes to effectively saying 'NO'. Being real and sincere in your communication is just as crucial as being honest and authentic.

Express yourself honestly and openly when you say 'NO'. Don't justify yourself or sugar-coat your answer. Being genuine fosters credibility and trust among colleagues. These characteristics are crucial components in promoting constructive dialogue and teamwork. Being genuine means that your words and deeds reflect who you are and what you stand for. Honesty is about being clear and sincere in your ideas, feelings and intentions.

Since they provide a sense of credibility and dependability, honesty and authenticity are crucial when it comes to saying 'NO'. Honest communication about your constraints, priorities and boundaries gives others clarity and transparency, which promotes mutual understanding and better decision-making. Insincerity increases the possibility of misunderstandings, animosity and trust erosion, all of which can damage relationships and reduce output.

It takes self-awareness and introspection to communicate with honesty and authenticity. It entails developing a thorough awareness of your own boundaries and beliefs, as well as the courage to boldly express them – even in awkward or difficult situations. You cannot hide behind a veneer or pretend to be someone you are not. The best way to communicate with honesty and authenticity is to cultivate self-awareness and mindfulness. Spend some time thinking about the ideas, emotions and driving forces behind your behaviour at work. Be truthful with yourself. In your interactions with other people, make an effort to communicate your ideas and sentiments openly and sincerely while simultaneously paying attention to their viewpoints and worries. Don't exaggerate your answers or inflate the truth – this will erode credibility and trust.

Maintain consistency between your words and deeds and coordinate them with your ideals and values. This calls for honesty and a determination to be loyal to who you are, even under trying circumstances. In addition to fostering a greater feeling of self-awareness and happiness in your own life, adopting honesty and sincerity in communication helps you develop strong relationships with others and earn their trust and respect. These attributes open doors to deeper bonds, authentic relationships and an existence free from needless obligations.

The capacity of precision and clarity to promote respect and understanding among people makes them essential in work situations. People who are open and honest about their limits, priorities and talents help others make better judgements and modify their expectations. This fosters an environment of trust and respect for one another because it communicates with honesty and integrity. Moreover, by avoiding the possible dangers of ambiguous or vague communication, such as dissatisfaction, resentment and mistrust, clarity and accuracy help to preserve the integrity of relationships.

Communication that is clear and precise is the result of carefully planning both the message's content and delivery. Before sharing your priorities and boundaries with others, it is first important to be clear about them yourself. Think carefully about why you are saying 'NO', and decide what is most important. After that, make sure your word choice is deliberate to convey a clear and succinct message. Using precise language and examples to support your arguments is a good way to achieve clarity. Instead of supporting your position using evasive or unclear language that could be interpreted differently, give precise and pertinent details. Furthermore, take into account the context and timing of your communication, as these may affect how your message is understood. To have a focused and polite talk about your limits and boundaries, it could be beneficial to arrange a private discussion or meeting with the person requesting it.

Listening to others

To create a workplace free from excessive duty, active listening is essential as it fosters empathy and mutual understanding. People can obtain important insights into the needs and expectations of others by carefully listening to their viewpoints and concerns. This enables them to respond in a kind and courteous manner.

During conversations, pay attention to what other people are saying. Before answering, consider their viewpoints. This promotes understanding and shows respect for their points of view. People who listen intently to others are better able to understand their underlying emotions and motivations. This makes it possible for people to respond with greater empathy since they can accept and validate other people's worries, even if they have to turn them down. By making sure that each person feels heard and respected during the communication process, active listening also aids in the avoidance of miscommunications and confrontations.

Being dependable and consistent

It takes self-control, accountability and a dedication to upholding the highest standards of professionalism and integrity to achieve consistency and dependability in communication. Setting up limits and priorities and following them through in all encounters is a good way to start. This means communicating expectations clearly and realistically with others to promote mutual understanding and alignment.

It's critical to dependably and promptly fulfil promises and obligations, despite any difficulties or setbacks. Efficient time management and organisational abilities are necessary for consistency and dependability. Setting and maintaining proper priorities for duties and responsibilities is crucial to meeting deadlines and controlling expectations. People can reduce their chance of overcommitting and make sure that their actions constantly correspond with their boundaries and priorities by maintaining organisation and taking the initiative to manage their workload and deadlines efficiently.

Additionally, being dependable and consistent means keeping lines of communication open and honest with others. To make sure that expectations are managed successfully, it's critical to convey changes in circumstances or the need to modify promises in a timely and transparent manner. People can lessen the effects of unforeseen changes and preserve mutual respect and trust in relationships by being honest about any limitations or restrictions.

Being receptive to feedback

Being receptive to criticism is crucial because it can help people become more self-aware at work. People can gain fresh perspectives and insights into their areas of strength and growth when they are open to receiving comments. By pointing out blind spots or areas of weakness that can impair their capacity to set limits or say 'NO' with confidence, constructive criticism can act as a catalyst for development.

Feedback is truly gold – it enables people to understand how their actions affect other people and modify their behaviour accordingly, which results in more fruitful relationships. Even though receiving criticism can be difficult or uncomfortable, approach it with an open mind, a willingness to listen, and an intention to learn from other people's viewpoints. Having a development mindset – which entails accepting challenges, asking for feedback and seeing setbacks as chances for improvement – is a practical way to become open to criticism. Actively seek out other opinions and provide a welcoming environment where such opinions are appreciated.

Receiving both constructive and positive comments is part of being open to input. Constructive feedback offers insightful information about areas for growth and progress, while positive feedback can bolster confidence and promote successful behaviours. It's critical to approach feedback with appreciation and interest as it offers a chance for both professional and personal growth. Show accountability and a commitment to

People can gain fresh perspectives and insights into their areas of strength and growth when they are open to receiving comments.

Darren Finkelstein

ongoing development by answering criticism with humility and a will to act on the new understandings.

A clever and straightforward method for saying 'NO'

In the course of researching this book, I got in touch with my long-time friend Callum Laing. Callum is a successful entrepreneur, author and investor. He is the founder and Chair of MBH Corporation PLC, and has sat on and advised many other boards privately and publicly for more than a decade. Callum set up the Veblen Director Programme in late 2022 due to frustration at how dysfunctional many boards are and how much talent was being overlooked for stupid reasons.[9]

I cannot imagine a more qualified, real-world person who has repeatedly said 'NO' to build his life of choice without obligation, especially when it comes to other entrepreneurs who are either pitching ideas to Callum for funding or just looking to pick his brain for easy solutions.

During our conversation, Callum revealed an incredibly clever and straightforward method he adopts for saying 'NO' to people without offending them, while returning the burden of responsibility right back to them. Callum said, 'I probably get five requests a week asking to catch up with people for coffee or "can I pick your brain" sessions.' Callum does not want to offend or seem uninterested, having been a young, enthusiastic entrepreneur himself. After all, Callum is a nice guy and doesn't want to be seen as an unsympathetic knob.

The reality is that Callum simply does not have spare time available to share with others. So, here's Callum's trick that he uses with great success.

His reply to everyone who asks is, 'Sounds great. I don't have any time this month, but tell me specifically what it is you would like to know, and I'll see if I can help.' Well, that does the job – a staggering 99% of the time, Callum will never hear back from

---

9   If you're interested in a board seat at some stage, please contact Callum Laing and his team at the Veblen Director Programme, which is a unique Training Program and Community for career-ambitious individuals and entrepreneurs. Check out: www.veblendirectors.com

them. Most folks who want to pick Callum's brain simply cannot be bothered doing the thinking necessary to articulate what it is they need! Callum says, 'So why should I give up my time to do their thinking? Saying no this way works well for me.'

Callum is exactly right, and it was only when it was used on Callum many years ago that he realised what a great and powerful statement it is. Since most of us assume the best in people, and we don't like letting others down, a statement like this takes the guilt off you (as the person saying 'NO') and puts the effort back on the other person.

For the tiny one percenter that does respond, most of the time Callum can answer in an email or direct them to someone better suited to respond, such as an expert in that area. No time is wasted, and there is a win–win outcome.

This is why successful people are very clear and succinct in their requests up-front, and would normally start by framing them in terms of what's in it for the other person, with clarity and precision.

'Lazy people can't be bothered to think that far ahead,' said Callum – and he's right!

A 'NO committee'

I discovered a very interesting study on saying 'NO' which was run by four scientists and published at www.nature.com. A group of mid-career environmental social scientists embarked on a year-long challenge to collectively decline 100 work-related requests.

This endeavour, born out of a desire to manage pandemic and career burnout, highlights the importance of saying 'NO' to maintain focus, productivity and mental health. By creating a 'no committee' among themselves, they aimed to support each other in making more selective commitments.

This research supports the idea that saying 'NO' can be beneficial for both individuals and organisations by helping to prioritise tasks and reduce burnout.

By putting these important lessons into practice, you can acquire the abilities needed to successfully negotiate workplace dynamics, uphold boundaries and put your own needs first while cultivating successful relationships and career advancement. In order to successfully negotiate workplace dynamics, this chapter emphasises the importance of creating boundaries, prioritising tasks and communicating effectively.

Top takeaways and lessons learned

☒ **Differentiating between assertiveness and aggression:** It's critical to recognise the difference between aggressiveness and assertiveness to preserve positive relationships and productive workplace interactions. You can avoid needless confrontation and promote cooperation, mutual respect and trust by setting boundaries in a forceful yet courteous manner.

☒ **Agreeing to responsibilities:** Effectively managing the ability to refuse requests while meeting obligations necessitates a calculated strategy.

☒ **Establishing mutual respect and trust:** Establishing a healthy work environment requires open communication to foster mutual respect and trust.

☒ **Active listening:** Effective communication, empathy and understanding are enhanced when co-workers' opinions and concerns are actively listened to.

☒ **Consistency and dependability:** Over time, credibility and trust are established by acting and communicating with consistency and reliability.

Chapter 6

Saying 'NO' in your daily life

Saying 'NO' more frequently is a habit that enables you to live more genuinely, aligning your everyday activities with your goals and basic values. This way of living places a strong emphasis on choosing consciously what is best for you, as opposed to giving in to peer pressure or other pressures. It involves claiming your independence and making thoughtful choices that provide you with a sense of fulfilment and direction. Saying 'NO' more frequently is about using judgement rather than being negative or obstructive. It entails assessing every demand, opportunity or request you receive to see if it fits with your values and aspirations. You can efficiently prioritise your time, energy and resources through this discernment process, ensuring that you are committed to activities that are truly important to you.

Saying 'NO' to an extra project at work that would put you over your head or delaying an invitation to a social gathering that doesn't interest you, for example, frees up time to engage in a hobby you enjoy. These actions preserve the quality of your current commitments and your individual wellbeing.

Setting clear boundaries and saying 'NO' more often are necessary for both good relationships and self-care. Establishing boundaries helps build relationships based on respect and

Making it a habit to say 'NO' more often will free you up to say 'YES' to chances, relationships and experiences that genuinely speak to your soul.

Darren Finkelstein

understanding by letting people know who you are and whether you are prepared to accept or engage with them. Knowing your boundaries helps you avoid burnout and overstretching yourself, which improves your general wellbeing and makes it possible for you to participate fully in the facets of life you have chosen to participate in.

Saying 'NO' more frequently is also a brave gesture that defies social conventions that associate success with busyness, the fear of missing out (FOMO) and the concern about disappointing other people. To resist these constant influences and select the best course for you – even if it means going down a less-travelled path – requires strength. This kind of courage results in a life that is an expression of who you truly are, not just a list of duties with no deeper significance.

Making it a habit to say 'NO' more often will free you up to say 'YES' to chances, relationships and experiences that genuinely speak to your soul. It makes room in your life for development, imagination and enquiry, guaranteeing that your 'YES' is based on sincere dedication and desire. By choosing carefully, you make every 'YES' more meaningful and fulfilling in life.

Workable techniques for daily activities

For those who want to live a life free from unnecessary obligation, incorporating 'NO' into their everyday life is crucial. The following methods enable people to uphold their boundaries, efficiently allocate their time and energy, and make sure that their day-to-day activities are consistent with their long-term objectives and fundamental beliefs. These methods are significant because they enable people to live intentionally, which helps them deal with the many possibilities and demands they face with purpose and clarity.

Setting priorities for responsibilities and tasks is a vital strategy. People can decide where to spend their time and energy by making a thorough assessment of what is most vital and urgent in their lives. This entails figuring out what fits and what doesn't with your goals, both personal and professional. For instance, it becomes easy to say 'NO' to needless social engagements or late work hours if spending time with family is your top priority.

Taking time to think about the ramifications of answering 'YES' or 'NO' enables people to evaluate how each choice fits into the larger scheme of their values and lives, so mindful contemplation before answering questions or seizing opportunities is another useful tactic. This introspection can involve weighing the possible time implications, the degree to which the request aligns with personal objectives, or the amount of mental or physical effort needed. Through thoughtful decision-making, people can steer clear of the reflexive 'YES' that frequently results in stress and overcommitment and instead make decisions that truly support their goals and wellbeing.

The ability to communicate effectively is another essential skill for practising saying 'NO'. It is easier to avoid misunderstandings and preserve good connections when you communicate a decision in a straightforward, courteous and firm way. This entails justifying 'NO' when it's appropriate, providing alternatives when feasible, and reaffirming your dedication to current goals. For example, while turning down a project at work, you could justify the choice by pointing out your existing responsibilities and recommend a co-worker who is capable of taking it on. When people communicate well, 'NO' becomes a careful and meaningful answer rather than a rejection or lack of interest.

Establishing and upholding sound limits is another crucial tactic. Boundaries define the extent to which people accept and interact on a personal and professional level. Respect is fostered when boundaries are openly discussed and clearly defined, and others assist in understanding your needs and expectations. Boundaries are essential for maintaining integrity, whether it's deciding not to participate in conversations that jeopardise your mental health or establishing strict work hours to avoid burnout.

Living by your principles is strengthened when you surround yourself with others who appreciate and respect your decisions. You can find support, guidance and empathy from this network, which can help you make clear judgements. Talking with people who value purposeful living about their experiences and methods can offer fresh insights and encouragement, strengthening your fortitude in the face of difficulties.

Creating an obligation-free existence requires integrating these practical strategies into everyday activities. They guarantee

When people communicate well, 'NO' becomes a careful and meaningful answer rather than a rejection or lack of interest.

Darren Finkelstein

that people can stay faithful to their beliefs and objectives by offering the framework and assistance required to intentionally traverse life's complications. People can live happy, purposeful, independent lives by setting boundaries, prioritising tasks, engaging in thoughtful introspection, communicating clearly and building supporting networks.

Affirmations and setting realistic objectives

Within the framework of saying 'NO', affirmations and realistic goal-setting are essential activities that provide people with the mental clarity and focus they need to make empowered decisions about what in their lives to accept or reject. The following exercises provide the groundwork for developing a sense of direction and self-awareness, which are essential for consciously and purposefully managing the many demands of life.

Positive and forceful remarks about yourself, or affirmations, are valuable for boosting confidence and self-esteem. They support your conviction that you have the freedom to make decisions that are in line with your goals and wellbeing. Your perspective can be changed by consistently using affirmations. Instead of instinctively responding 'YES' when something does not serve your highest benefit, you can say 'NO' with confidence. An affirmation like, 'I have the power to choose what aligns with my values', for example, can give someone the confidence to turn down a lucrative employment offer that would require them to compromise on moral or ethical principles. By cultivating inner strength and conviction, this helps people stick to their convictions in the face of outside pressure.

Setting reasonable goals is equally significant because it gives you a clear idea of what you want to accomplish and helps you decide which opportunities and requests fit these goals and which don't. A realistic goal serves as a compass, pointing you in the direction of decisions that will get you closer to your goals. It is simpler to recognise and say 'NO' to commitments or diversions that could take time and energy away from your goals when your objectives are well defined. When someone establishes a goal to get healthier, for instance, declining social invitations that interfere with their exercise regimen or food preferences can help them stay on track.

Combining affirmations with doable goals fosters a proactive as opposed to a reactive attitude towards life's choices. People can forge their own path with a distinct vision and a strong sense of self, rather than being carried away by the tide of expectations and demands from outside sources. Being proactive is crucial for creating a life of choice because it allows people to choose the relationships and activities that truly improve their lives and make them feel happy and fulfilled.

A cycle of positive reinforcement is further facilitated when realistic targets are created in conjunction with affirmations. Reaching goals increases self-assurance and validates the power of affirmations, resulting in a positive feedback loop that enables people to better manage their lives. Saying 'NO' to inappropriate requests and 'YES' to chances that align with one's basic principles and objectives is encouraged by this cycle.

Affirmations and realistic goal-setting are powerful tools on the path to saying 'NO' and creating an autonomous, choice-filled existence. They provide people with the guidance, clarity and self-assurance they need to make choices that are consistent with their beliefs and wellbeing. People can design a life that is full of joy and significance, in addition to being in line with who they truly are.

Your point of view is legitimate

It can be a liberating sensation to stand alone and hold a different opinion to the majority. It necessitates a deep sense of conviction and self-awareness that enables you to authentically negotiate the intricacies of cultural expectations. Saying 'NO' and building a life of choice without obligation means more than just turning down an offer; it means standing by your principles, your priorities, and your right to make your own decisions. The rewards of maintaining your integrity and self-respect are abundant on this route, but it can also be difficult at times due to strong social pressure to fit in.

Being the only one with an opposing viewpoint in a crowded field calls for bravery and tenacity. It entails accepting the awkwardness of being different and the potential for mis-interpretation or judgement. However, it is this very willingness to stay true to yourself that develops inner clarity and power. It says volumes about your commitment to living genuinely when you choose to stick to your values even when you are alone in a world where comfort frequently correlates with consensus. It is evidence of the strength of uniqueness and the significance of following your true path without regard to approval from others.

Being by yourself can be an inspiration to others who might have similar feelings but lack the courage to voice them. They may be motivated by your example to speak up and accept their own opinions. This knock-on effect emphasises the value of personal conviction and how it contributes to the development of a true variety of opinions and behaviour in society. Standing alone is a journey that is far from lonely, even though it is solitary. It helps you gain a better knowledge of both the world and yourself by highlighting the power that comes from leading an authentic life.

In the end, allowing yourself to be a lone voice comes down to putting your truth ahead of the convenience of fitting in. It's about accepting that, despite its deviation from the usual, your point of view is legitimate. Being able to accept yourself is essential to creating a life that is characterised by freedom and choice rather than duty. Not only are you expressing your decisions by embracing the strength of 'NO' and standing by yourself, but you are also creating an environment free from the demands of others that would otherwise stifle your authenticity.

Creating a network of support

While having the backing of others is certainly good, it's not always attainable. If this situation arises, don't just give in and say 'YES' to appease others.

To address your reasons for saying 'NO' in a range of scenarios, it would be beneficial to reach out to your support network for supportive advice, enlightening discussion, and other helpful techniques. It's beneficial to go over how you set your limits because handling different relationships and circumstances requires a sophisticated approach.

In the end, allowing yourself to be a lone voice comes down to putting your truth ahead of the convenience of fitting in.

Darren Finkelstein

Through sharing experiences, effective communication techniques and strategies with others in their support system, people can develop the skills necessary to express 'NO' clearly and compassionately with respect and empathy, thus reducing misunderstandings and encouraging mutual admiration. Keep in mind that professional development and continuous, regular training can be helpful in this field.

You may inspire and encourage people through your network and in your organisation by demonstrating leadership by example. We need more leaders to lead from the front. Observing peers and mentors successfully managing their lives via intention and choice can be incredibly inspiring. It serves as a tangible reminder of the benefits and viability of living a true life and making choices that are consistent with one's true nature. Seeing others thrive by saying 'NO' to commitments that don't benefit them inspires people to apply the same ideas to their own lives, and reaffirms that it is both extremely rewarding and feasible.

Having a support network in place may also reduce the chance of feeling alone or alienated as a result of making choices that go against social norms or expectations. Knowing that others value and experience similar things as you do helps you develop a sense of community. This feeling of belonging may be quite empowering and comforting, proving that you're not the only one who prefers to live a life of choice. This communal empowerment promotes a more confident, compassionate and open approach to creating a life that truly reflects one's values, aspirations and needs.

Saying 'NO' becomes a deliberate instrument for growth: Andrew Griffiths, international bestselling author and global speaker

Saying 'NO' becomes a deliberate instrument for growth and personal development in the context of entrepreneurship and business development, rather than just a reaction.

The insights offered by Andrew Griffiths, an international bestselling author and global speaker, renowned for his in-depth knowledge of business dynamics and successful tactics, are provided in this section. Andrew offers a sophisticated viewpoint on the idea of saying 'NO' in both personal and professional circumstances. His extensive expertise includes writing 14 books and having an impact on audiences in 65 countries.

Andrew responded to the book's title *NO* by realising its utter necessity right away. Andrew sees that when we say 'NO', we are able to express 'YES' to what is really important. This acknowledgement is a result of his own struggle with the difficulties of refusing, which has been fuelled by a propensity for people-pleasing, a fear of rejection, and erroneous ideas about obligation. However, it was by facing these obstacles that Andrew realised how important 'NO' is for reaching important life and professional goals.

The workings of 'NO'

For Andrew, there were a few crucial tactics that helped him go from being unable to refuse to being comfortable saying 'NO':

☒ **The use of time as a buffer by imposing a delay:** By allowing himself time to respond, Andrew was able to consider requests carefully and make sure that his answers reflected his goals and values.

☒ **Using a checklist:** Creating a decision-making checklist helped him weigh opportunities against his existing goals and obligations.

☒ **Acquiring knowledge via observation:** Andrew developed a template for saying 'NO' without destroying relationships by seeing and copying how others politely and successfully turned down requests.

For Andrew, learning to say 'NO' resulted in profound transformations that signified a move towards greater integrity and personal autonomy. It created an environment free from guilt or animosity, allowing him to fully commit to his decisions. It also emphasised how crucial it is to protect one's integrity and personal brand, especially in the business world where chances abound but aren't always in line with one's path.

Advice for up-and-coming business owners

Andrew emphasises how crucial it is to learn how to say 'NO' early in the entrepreneurial process. His guidance for aspiring business owners is to master the skill of saying 'NO' while weighing it against the discernment to know whether an opportunity is worthwhile. He stresses how important it is to match prospects with one's present business requirements, and he exhorts business owners to avoid becoming sidetracked from their key goals by staying alert.

The strategic application of 'NO' becomes a vital ability in the process of creating a meaningful life and business, allowing people to forge paths that truly align with their aspirations for achievement.

Andrew's best advice on saying 'NO':

☒ **Choose a method that suits your needs.** Andrew adores the concept of biding his time until he has more time to think things through and make a decision, instead of saying 'NO' outright.

☒ **Create your checklist.** Andrew and I have much in common on this front. Andrew, like me, weighs each offer against his personal and professional 'checklist' to make sure he stays true to his mission, his path and his objectives. He doesn't want to be sidetracked by bright lights that divert his valuable time and resources from the agreed-upon work at hand or goal.

☒ **Observe others.** Learn how to politely refuse by observing others and how they respectfully and politely say 'NO' and explain their reasons. Make sure the person receiving the 'NO' doesn't feel abandoned and rejected. The request just does not align with your priorities, emphasis, or schedule. Explain your reasons for saying 'NO'. Emphasise that this is not personal.

CHAPTER 6 REVIEW

Saying 'NO' more frequently is essential for living a genuine and fulfilling life, aligning your activities with your personal values and goals. It involves conscious decision-making, prioritising time and energy, and establishing clear boundaries to maintain wellbeing and meaningful commitments. This encourages self-awareness and courage, enabling you to resist societal pressures and choose paths that resonate with your true self. Effective communication and support networks further aid in this process, fostering respect and understanding in relationships. Ultimately, saying 'NO' allows for a more intentional and purpose-driven life.

Top takeaways and lessons learned

- **Conscious decision-making:** Saying 'NO' helps align daily activities with personal values and goals, ensuring decisions are made thoughtfully rather than after succumbing to external pressures.

- **Prioritisation:** By assessing requests against your values and aspirations, you can prioritise time and energy for activities that truly matter to you.

- **Boundary setting:** Establishing clear boundaries promotes wellbeing and respectful relationships, preventing burnout and overcommitment.

- **Courage and self-awareness:** Saying 'NO' requires strength to defy social conventions and the courage to choose a path that reflects your true self.

- **Effective communication:** Clear, courteous and firm communication of decisions helps avoid misunderstandings and maintains positive relationships.

- **Support networks:** Building and utilising support networks provides guidance and encouragement, reinforcing the practice of saying 'NO' and fostering a sense of community.

Chapter 7

Changing your own behaviour with 'NO'

Recognising the power of saying 'NO' enables people to take charge of their lives and live more intentionally, aligning with their long-term goals. Fundamentally, being able to say 'NO' gives people the strength to defy cultural pressures, impulsive choices and the constant barrage of marketing campaigns meant to change their consumption habits.

Matching your daily decisions with your long-term goals

For a number of reasons, making the deliberate decision to say 'NO' is essential to achieving long-term goals. First of all, we all have a limited supply of resources, time and energy. Saying 'YES' to everything that is presented to you has the potential to quickly spiral into overcommitment, in which your efforts in areas that are genuinely important to you are of lower quality and efficacy due to the excessive distribution of your limited resources. Saying 'NO' to opportunities that don't fit with your long-term

Freedom on the inside comes when validation from the outside doesn't matter.

Richie Norton

objectives helps you safeguard these resources and make sure they're used for things that are genuinely meaningful and have the potential to make a big difference in your long-term success and fulfilment.

Strategic refusal helps in maintaining focus. In a world filled with distractions and endless opportunities, maintaining a clear aim on your long-term objectives can be challenging. Saying 'NO' acts as a filter, helping to ward off distractions and keep your actions aligned with your goals. This alignment is crucial for progress, as it enables you to dedicate more time and energy to your priorities, thereby accelerating your journey towards achieving them.

Saying 'NO' is fundamental to setting and respecting your own boundaries, which is essential for personal wellbeing and mental health. It communicates to others that your time, energy and priorities are valuable, fostering mutual respect and understanding. This aspect of strategic refusal not only contributes to a healthier work–life balance but also enhances your self-esteem and decision-making confidence, as you actively choose which commitments are worth your investment.

Are the choices you make on a daily basis in line with your long-term objectives? You are spending valuable time being sidetracked if they aren't.

Daily decisions must be in line with long-term objectives to guarantee that every action taken advances those objectives. Since time is a finite resource, every choice we make that pulls us from our goals costs us time that could have been used to make real progress. Distractions and instant rewards frequently cause this misalignment by luring us away from the methodical pursuit of our long-term goals.

Learning to say 'NO' is an essential discipline in living a life that has meaning. It acts as a gatekeeper, keeping our time and energy from being depleted by unimportant duties or responsibilities. Saying 'NO' to distractions demonstrates our dedication to our objectives and the strategy we have selected to achieve them. This deliberate approach, which eliminates the clutter of unnecessary activities, helps to preserve mental clarity, lower stress levels and boost productivity.

Living purposefully is about making sure that the choices we make daily are consistent with our long-term objectives. It's about maximising our limited resources to create a meaningful and successful existence. Saying 'NO' to distractions means embracing what we want instead of just avoiding what we don't want. It's about writing the story of the life we choose to live, one that is full of meaning and free from regrets over time squandered on the unimportant.

It takes intentionality and discipline to match our daily decisions with our long-term activities. It all starts with having a clear purpose; we need to know why we are pursuing these long-term objectives and how to articulate them to ourselves. With this vision in place, we can divide these objectives into more manageable, practical tasks that we can include into our everyday schedules. Planning and prioritising our daily activities to make sure they directly contribute to our larger aims is part of this process. To help with this, we can use digital apps, planners and to-do lists to keep track of our goals and progress.

At the same time, we need to have the self-control to stick to our goals in the face of distractions and temptations. This is when knowing when to say 'NO' becomes essential. We purposefully withhold our time and effort from demands, tasks and activities that do not further our main objectives. It also entails establishing limits and being prepared to defend our time with firmness.

Two further essential elements of this alignment process are reflection and review. We can determine whether we are on track and what needs to be adjusted by routinely reflecting on our activities and results. This might be a weekly review to get ready for the next week, or it could be a daily reflection each evening. It all comes down to being flexible enough to adjust as circumstances demand, and making constant, small changes.

Self-awareness is important because it helps us establish an atmosphere that supports concentrated work by helping us identify our periods of productivity, our motivators and our routines. For instance, we can arrange our most crucial chores for the morning if we know that this is when we are most productive.

Are the choices you make on a daily basis in line with your long-term objectives? You are spending valuable time being sidetracked if they aren't.

Darren Finkelstein

Saying 'NO' to conspicuous consumption

To comply with Australian government regulations, as well as my personal desire for complete transparency, I must state before I begin this section that the financial information and strategies shared in this book are intended for general educational and informational purposes only.[10]

Now that's out of the way, let's get on with it!

In a society where marketing and advertising are everywhere, resistance to these pressures is powerful. The ability to say 'NO' allows people to withstand the compelling and frequently deceptive strategies used by marketers to encourage consumption. Resisting the need to give in to manufactured desires enables people to make decisions that are more consistent with their own needs and values.

This opposition is important for many reasons. Peer pressure, fashion and the need for social acceptance are just a few examples of the social variables that have an impact on consumer behaviour through social pressures and trends. Individuals who choose not to participate in these trends can uphold their integrity and make decisions that are authentically theirs instead of fitting in with social norms.

Two key components of consumer behaviour that cause regret and unstable finances are the inability to control one's impulses and impulsive purchases. Saying 'NO' improves impulse control and promotes more careful and considerate shopping selections. This 'NO' promotes a greater sense of personal fulfilment and wellness in addition to being in line with long-term financial objectives.

The power of 'NO' and sustainable and ethical consumption go hand in hand in fostering these values. Through their refusal to buy items that hurt the environment or are produced unethically, consumers have the power to influence business behaviour and make the world more equitable and sustainable. Saying 'NO' promotes conscientious consumption. Consumer decisions have a big impact in an era of ethical dilemmas and environmental disasters. People can influence market trends and corporate

---

10   Please read the disclaimer on page 229.

behaviour by driving demand for more responsible products and services by refusing to support unethical enterprises or unsustainable methods. Thus, individual acts are in line with the interests of the group as a whole, supporting larger societal and environmental objectives.

A key component of financial wellbeing is having the ability to say 'NO'. People can direct their resources towards things that are important to them, including investing in personal growth, saving for the future or supporting organisations they are passionate about by declining pointless purchases or investments. This deliberate distribution of resources not only helps them achieve their long-term objectives but also gives them a feeling of contentment and purpose.

Stress, worry and a feeling of being overburdened can result from the demand placed on us by society to continuously interact, consume and comply with expectations. A more balanced and controllable lifestyle can be created by setting boundaries and choosing not to give in to these pressures.

It is impossible to overestimate the importance of saying 'NO' when it comes to budgeting and financial planning, since it has a direct impact on one's capacity to attain financial independence and stability. This habit is essential to developing a strategic personal finance management plan, as being able to turn down some expenses is critical to staying in line with one's long-term financial goals.

Saying 'NO' performs several crucial functions, including enforcing self-control, curbing impulsive spending and giving priority to the distribution of resources towards objectives that are truly valuable to the individual, such as debt repayment, retirement savings and educational investments. A sense of empowerment and control over one's financial future are fostered by this practice. People who deliberately choose not to give in to impulse purchases or social pressure to spend money live lives of financial responsibility and independence. This freedom provides the release from the stress and limitations of living payday to payday or being burdened by needless debt, in addition to having the ability to spend money whenever one pleases. Saying 'NO' to financial pressures is ultimately a statement of intent – a pledge to achieve financial independence,

Intentional living is a lifestyle. It is a holistic way to show up for the things that matter most in your life.

Lora de Vries

personal development and the realisation of one's greatest goals and values, free from constraints.

Saying 'NO' to unhealthy habits

Saying 'NO' to unhealthy habits represents a critical step towards establishing a life of choice, marked by autonomy and freedom. This decision has profound implications for both physical and mental wellbeing, acting as a catalyst for positive change. Unhealthy habits, if not controlled and managed appropriately, can kill you – everything ranging from poor dietary choices, excessive alcohol consumption, smoking, substance abuse and physical inactivity to excessive stress without adequate coping mechanisms.

The act of saying 'NO' to these habits is fundamentally an act of self-care and respect, signalling a commitment to prioritising one's health and wellbeing above immediate gratification or societal pressures.

The importance of this decision extends beyond the immediate health benefits. Psychologically, it reinforces a sense of self-efficacy and control, vital components of mental resilience and happiness. It reflects an individual's capacity to make decisions that align with their long-term goals and values, rather than succumbing to momentary desires or external expectations. This self-directed approach to living ensures that one's life trajectory is determined by conscious choice rather than passive acquiescence to unhealthy patterns.

Saying 'NO' to unhealthy habits is integral to building a life devoid of unwanted obligations – to illness, to financial burdens associated with healthcare, and to the emotional and physical constraints imposed by poor health. It is a declaration of independence, affirming one's ability to shape their destiny and live according to their own terms. In essence, this choice embodies the broader principle of living intentionally, where every decision is made with awareness of its long-term impact.

Ultimately, saying 'NO' to unhealthy habits is not just about rejecting negative behaviours but about embracing a vision of life that is rich in health, fulfilment and autonomy. It's about making choices that enable you to lead a vibrant, active life, unencumbered by the limitations that these habits can impose. The power of 'NO' is transformative, offering a pathway to a life defined by purpose, freedom, and the pursuit of personal wellbeing. Saying 'NO' to bad behaviours is essential to paving the way for better physical and mental health, acting as a cornerstone for long-term fulfilment and personal development. It is ultimately about actively choosing a life where physical and mental wellbeing are prioritised, which enables the realisation of long-term goals and the achievement of a meaningful, fulfilling existence.

Saying 'YES' to a balanced and healthy lifestyle

Breaking free from unhealthy habits through the power of 'NO' isn't just about avoiding negative outcomes. This lifestyle decision is important for many reasons, all of which are firmly anchored in the desire for fulfilment, longevity and wellbeing. A balanced lifestyle incorporates mental and physical wellbeing, regular exercise, a healthy diet and enough sleep to create a state of health that promotes the best possible functioning of the body and mind.

This deliberate way of life is essential for several reasons.

It increases life expectancy and establishes the groundwork for strong physical health by lowering the chance of chronic conditions like obesity, diabetes and heart disease. It involves avoiding bad habits like smoking, binge drinking and sedentarism, and opting instead for meals and activities that support the body. This proactive approach to health involves choosing to say 'NO' to quick decisions that could cause long-term harm in favour of decisions that lead to vitality and wellness.

A balanced lifestyle is essential for mental and emotional wellbeing in addition to physical wellbeing. Regular physical activity and eating a nutrient-dense diet have been demonstrated to improve mood, reduce symptoms of anxiety and depression, and improve cognitive performance. People who adopt this lifestyle say 'NO' to the tension and mental exhaustion that frequently result from leading an imbalanced life. It is a declaration that mental wellbeing is equally important to physical wellbeing and should be treated with the same respect.

A balanced lifestyle is a must for creating an obligation-free, choice-driven life. It represents a choice to be free to follow one's passions, objectives and dreams with all of one's might rather than letting bad health decisions weigh you down. It is putting long-term contentment and satisfaction ahead of fleeting joys or obediently adhering to harmful social conventions.

A healthy lifestyle promotes self-efficacy and a sense of control over one's fate. It is a daily confirmation of one's capacity to make choices consistent with long-term goals and personal values. Living intentionally, in which every decision is made with a clear idea of the kind of life one wants to lead, is based on this empowerment. Adopting a balanced and healthy lifestyle is essentially a strong 'NO' to the forces that aim to compromise our autonomy and health. It is an expression of a strong belief that the decisions we make have a direct impact on the quality of our lives and a dedication to self-respect.

Saying 'NO' to technology overwhelm

In an age where digital connection can invade every part of our daily lives, learning to say 'NO' when it comes to technology is essential to carving out a life without obligation. The capacity to create boundaries with technology involves more than just refusing to utilise specific tools or platforms; it also involves consciously deciding where to focus our attention and efforts to achieve our long-term goals.

Saying 'NO' to needless digital consumption is crucial for a number of deep reasons in a world where social media feeds, continual notifications and the lure of infinite information abound.

Setting boundaries with technology helps people recover their time and attention, which are frequently broken up by the constant demands of the digital world. This time that has been recovered is essential for engaging in pursuits that support one's objectives and moral principles, such as community service, personal growth and relationship building. By deciding to use technology on our terms, we free up our time and energy for activities that are important to us and help us achieve our long-term goals.

Our mental health and general wellbeing may be impacted by digital weariness, tension, and even anxiety brought on by the continual connectedness and deluge of information. Saying 'NO' to excessive digital involvement can help people counteract these negative impacts and cultivate a mental state that is better suited for introspection, creativity and concentrated work. When it comes to making choices and acting in ways that support our long-term goals, this mental clarity is crucial.

Setting technological limitations also makes a strong statement against the culture of instant gratification that digital platforms support. It promotes a patient and persistent mindset, which are necessary for reaching important, long-term objectives. In contrast to the transient gratification and fast fixes provided by the digital world, pursuing worthwhile goals frequently calls for consistent effort and attention. We develop the resiliency and resolve required to overcome the obstacles present in any meaningful endeavour by avoiding the lure of constant digital involvement.

Technology boundaries also make it possible to engage with people on a deeper, more meaningful level. Setting a higher priority on in-person contacts can result in more satis-fying relationships in a time when digital communication frequently trumps face-to-face communication. In turn, these connections help and encourage us to pursue our long-term objectives, enhancing our path to a purposeful and independent existence.

Saying 'NO' to unrestrained technology use is a powerful habit for achieving self-mastery. It represents a deliberate decision to take charge of our surroundings as opposed to allowing them to dominate us. Beyond using technology, this self-control affects other facets of our lives, where establishing limits is essential for development and success. It involves creating a life free from the external demands imposed by the digital world, one that expresses our deepest beliefs and goals.

The power of 'NO' in technology boundaries is, in essence, about living consciously and accomplishing our long-term

By deciding to use technology on our terms, we free up our time and energy for activities that are important to us and help us achieve our long-term goals.

Darren Finkelstein

goals – it goes beyond simply setting screen time limits. It gives us the ability to concentrate on the things that really count, improves our relationships, builds resilience, and supports mental and emotional health as well as self-discipline.

Saying 'NO' to the excesses of the digital era is, from this perspective, a significant statement of our autonomy and a critical first step towards creating a life free from obligations.

Disconnecting in a hyperconnected world

In a time when staying connected all the time is the standard, learning to say 'NO' and disconnecting can be a key strategy for achieving long-term goals and leading an intentional life. In our hyperconnected world, there is a constant stream of notifications, messages and updates vying for our attention. This might cause us to lose concentration and become less engaged in activities or projects that are in line with our long-term goals. By saying 'NO' to this never-ending connectedness, we can take back our time and focus it on things that actually help us reach our objectives. This promotes productivity and the accomplishment of worthwhile goals.

The constant demand on our attention impedes our ability to work with focus and to reflect and think introspectively – two crucial processes for knowing who we are, what we want out of life, and how we want it to go. Cutting digital ties gives us the mental room we need to reassess our principles, hone our future goals, and come up with plans on how to get there. We frequently discover clarity about our genuine goals and the will to pursue them during these silent times of detachment.

Maintaining emotional and mental wellbeing is another important benefit of disconnecting. Stress, worry and a feeling of being overloaded can result from the constant onslaught of information and the pressure to always be present. These mental states are incompatible with the consistent work needed to accomplish long-term objectives.

Disconnecting also improves the calibre of our exchanges and relationships. As more meaningful, in-person contacts are replaced by digital communication, the depth of our ties suffers. We create space for deeper, more fulfilling partnerships that offer support and encouragement as we work towards our long-term goals by saying 'NO' to shallow digital interactions. These connections, which are based on sincerity and common experiences, serve as the foundation for a meaningful and choice-filled life.

The act of disconnecting represents the more general idea of living deliberately. It symbolises a conscious decision to refuse to allow outside influences to determine the cadence and subject matter of our lives. This self-determination is empowering because it affirms our agency to live our lives in accordance with our highest goals and convictions rather than the expectations and demands of a global community.

Saying 'NO' to unplugging in a hyperconnected society is a powerful way to take back control of our lives, and is not just a way to cope with digital overload. It strengthens our resolve to live meaningfully, helps us to concentrate on the important things in life, promotes personal development and wellbeing, and strengthens our bonds with one another. Disconnection gives us the room and perspective we need to resolutely pursue our long-term goals and create a life of our own.

Information overload and social media management

To set long-term goals and create a life of conscious choice free from the unintentional obligations that these digital phenomena frequently involve, it is crucial to learn how to say 'NO' to information overload and to social media usage. It is not only about objecting to content or limiting social media use in a superficial way. The causes of this are complex and multidimensional, intricately linked to what it means to be an individual in the digital age and to be in control of your destiny.

Overindulgence in social media can seriously clog our mental landscape, making it harder to understand what is actually important. Because the human mind has a limited amount of cognitive bandwidth, processing, reflecting and constructively integrating large amounts of information might be hampered. Saying 'NO' to this onslaught allows us to protect our mental space, which facilitates better decision-making, clearer thinking and a stronger focus on pursuits that are consistent with our values and deeper aspirations. Establishing and achieving long-term goals requires this clarity.

Our sense of fulfillment and progress towards our goals can be undermined by the constant flow of information and the dynamics of social media, which frequently promote a culture of comparison and immediate gratification. Specifically, social media sites have the power to warp our sense of fulfilment and accomplishment by constantly showcasing the best parts of other people's lives, which can make us feel inadequate or impatient with our own path. By embracing the power of 'NO', we can distance ourselves from these counterproductive comparisons, focus on our own journeys, and recognise the inherent worth of each of our distinct goals and accomplishments.

Setting boundaries is a fundamental skill for any long-term endeavour, and the discipline needed to control information intake and social media use is an essential exercise in this regard. Establishing and upholding these limits fortifies our determination to say 'NO' to distractions and diversions in other spheres of our lives, in addition to aiding with digital landscape navigation.

Finding calm in the age of constant connectivity

In this time of perpetual connectedness, the ability to say 'NO' is valuable if you want to carve out areas of peace and quiet amid the digital chaos. This refusal is not just a denial; it is a deep declaration of independence.

The constant barrage of digital noise that permeates much of our contemporary lives frequently causes us to feel stressed and anxious as we try to keep up with the fast-paced online world. We give ourselves the chance to experience peace and quiet when we choose to unplug. This calmness gives us the mental clarity and emotional strength we need to face life's obstacles and remain faithful to our long-term goals, making it more than just a luxury for our mental and emotional health.

We can re-establish a connection with both the material world and our inner selves by saying 'NO' to continual connect-ivity. It creates room for introspection, enabling us to consider

Overindulgence in social media can seriously clog our mental landscape.

our objectives, re-evaluate our values, and consider the course of our lives without being distracted by outside noise. This self-examination is crucial to ensuring our long-term goals are genuinely in accordance with our basic principles and aren't unduly impacted by the passing fads and viewpoints that are widely shared online.

Also, by exercising our right to say 'NO', we give ourselves control over how we live our digital lives and refuse to be carried along by the tide of technology. This empowerment strengthens our capacity to set limits and make decisions in all spheres of life, not just virtual ones. It's an essential ability for anyone hoping to create a life of choice where commitments are made consciously and individual autonomy is maintained.

Saying 'NO' when necessary can help you find serenity in an era of continual connectivity and foster deeper, more meaningful relationships. Setting the importance of in-person relationships above digital ones creates a sense of community and belonging that is essential to your social welfare.

'NO', don't click that link!

The ability to say 'NO' when it comes to cybersecurity – specifically, the disciplined restraint to avoid clicking on untrusted links – is a critical component of protecting one's digital life. This deliberate refusal is a sign of a larger dedication to caution, self-preservation and alertness in an increasingly digital society, rather than just a defensive move against possible cyberthreats. This position has far-reaching consequences that affect privacy and personal security.

There is plenty of risk in the digital sphere that aims to jeopardise financial assets, personal information and general security. These threats range from malware and phishing schemes to more advanced cyberattacks. A malicious link can cause everything from minor inconveniences to major disruptions.

Saying 'NO' to the temptation to click on untrusted links, even if it looks like a real email from the bank, helps people practise digital hygiene, which safeguards their online assets and identity. The self-control needed to suppress these cravings develops a critical thinking and mindfulness mindset – attributes that are extremely beneficial outside of the cybersecurity domain. Vigilant examination of digital content, suspicion of offers that seem too good to be true, and the practice of confirming sources before interacting with them are all behaviours that improve one's ability to use judgement and foresight when navigating the internet and other spheres of life. By encouraging a proactive rather than reactive response to opportunities and difficulties, this mentality supports the pursuit of long-term goals by empowering people to make choices that are consistent with their beliefs and goals.

Saying 'NO' in this situation also signifies an assertion of control over one's use of digital media. It represents an awareness that not all content is produced with the user's best interests in mind inside the enormous, linked web of digital information. People take charge of their digital world by picking and choosing what they interact with, creating an online experience that enhances rather than detracts from their long-term objectives and wellbeing. In a time when digital platforms and algorithms are more and more attempting to influence user behaviour, this control is essential for preserving a sense of autonomy.

Last but not least, learning to love the power of 'NO' in cyber-security embodies the larger idea of individual accountability in a globalised society. It recognises that although we might not be able to influence other people's intentions, we do have a great deal of power over how we react to the digital world.

Saying 'NO' to strengthen your relationships

The paradoxical use of 'NO' in relationships highlights the need to strike a careful balance between one's limits and the interdependence of interpersonal interactions. Saying 'NO' shows respect for one's boundaries and requirements, as well as a sound sense of self-awareness. It is a crucial part of self-care and personal integrity since it communicates an individual's awareness of their own abilities, priorities and values.

Relationships can be greatly strengthened by this demarcation since it promotes integrity, openness and respect. The basis of mutual respect and trust that is established when people can articulate their boundaries without fear of criticism or retaliation is essential for every healthy relationship. This degree of transparency makes sure that exchanges and obligations are made voluntarily and happily rather than out of duty, which helps to keep the relationship healthy and avoid resentment.

On the other hand, having to say 'NO' can also highlight and expose underlying conflicts and miscommunications about expectations. Feelings of hurt, bewilderment or estrangement may result from what is viewed as rejection or a lack of desire to engage in the connection. A 'NO' can be misconstrued as a lack of concern or commitment, especially in partnerships where communication and mutual understanding are not well established. This could undermine the trust and intimacy between the parties. This misunderstanding underlines how important communication is in explaining the rationale for one's boundaries and choices. What is meant to be a self-preservation measure could be misinterpreted as animosity or apathy without open communication and an appreciation of one another's viewpoints, straining or even ending the partnership.

Negotiating the complexity brought forth by expressing 'NO' requires strong communication and respect. Open communication, empathy and a sincere attempt to comprehend one another's needs and viewpoints must be prioritised by both partners for a relationship to survive the possible difficulties presented by this paradox. Maintaining the delicate balance between respecting individual boundaries and fostering interpersonal connections takes deliberate effort.

Saying 'NO' when handled well may be a technique for building mutual respect and understanding, which helps a relationship develop and endure. However, when done incorrectly, it can cause miscommunication and conflict, under-scoring the complex and significant role that boundaries play in interpersonal relationships.

Saying 'NO' in any relationship shows that a relationship's strength lies not only in its ability to work together and agree on things but also in its ability to negotiate and respect boundaries and differences. Depending on the pillars on which the relationship is based and the willingness of both sides to have an honest, frank, and caring conversation, expressing 'NO' can either strengthen or undermine it.

Saying 'NO' to boost accountability

The power of saying 'NO' is sometimes underestimated in a society where we are continuously being pushed in the direction of 'YES'. Saying 'NO' isn't just a matter of preference in the context of personal and professional development, though; it's also the oxygen that keeps the flame of accountability burning. It's time for us now to explore the benefits of saying 'NO' and why it's essential for fostering an accountable culture.

The idea that saying 'NO' is the 'oxygen to accountability' captures the crucial role that refusing offers plays in promoting an environment of accountability and integrity in both the personal and professional spheres. This analogy emphasises how, in the same way that oxygen is necessary for humans and other life forms to survive, saying 'NO' gives the practice of 'accountability' life. Saying 'NO' is a strong declaration of one's boundaries, priorities, and – above all – a commitment to honouring one's morals and obligations. It's not just about rejecting or denying.

'NO' is an essential weapon for claiming control over one's decisions and actions when creating a life of choice free from obligation. It enables people to deliberately select the relationships, activities and commitments that support their values and aspirations and those that don't. Selective participation is essential to accountability since it entails accepting responsibility for one's decisions and the results they produce. Saying 'NO' to things that take away from their objectives or don't fulfil their purpose is a proactive way for people to take charge of their lives and travel in the direction they want them to go.

Think about the situation where a professional accepts an extra duty, although she is already overburdened with her present projects. In this case, saying 'NO' means recognising her abilities and pledging to uphold the standard of her current tasks. Saying 'NO' is a responsibility exercise that keeps her from overcommitting and underdelivering, which could damage her reputation and project results.

By saying 'NO', you set boundaries that are unambiguous and necessary for efficient accountability. Setting boundaries helps people clarify the extent of their duties and make the distinction between what they are responsible for and what is outside their domain. By establishing these boundaries with a firm 'NO', people can concentrate on doing their best to keep their word and build a culture of trust and dependability among their peers, co-workers and personal connections.

Saying 'NO' is an expression of introspection and self-awareness, which are essential elements of accountability. It necessitates that people continually assess their limitations, skills and priorities. Through self-reflection, individuals can make sure that their commitment to duties and obligations is appropriate and that it is motivated by their goals, both personal and professional.

'NO' is essentially the breath of accountability because it gives people the freedom to live deliberately, make decisions that are authentically theirs, and accept full responsibility for their deeds. It is an affirmation of their devotion to their ideals and objectives, guaranteeing that each 'YES' is a step closer to realising their promises and ambitions. Saying 'NO' becomes an essential habit for anyone trying to create a life of choice that is free of unjustified responsibility and marked by intentional engagement.

The essence of accountability

Being accountable means taking responsibility for your choices, commitments and tasks and being responsible for their outcomes. It's an assurance to both yourself and other people that you will keep your word, fulfil your responsibilities, and take accountability for your deeds. But without the capacity to refuse, real accountability is unattainable. It takes bravery to set boundaries and acknowledge when something doesn't fit with your values or abilities. It's not only about accepting responsibility for the good times.

You gotta make it a priority to make your priorities a priority.

Richie Norton

Let us ensure that we all have a clear understanding of what 'accountability' actually means. Most individuals can't even spell the dreaded 'A' word correctly and don't truly comprehend what it means, even though its use has significantly increased.

The usage of the word 'accountability' in business has seen a notable increase over the past five years. This rise is closely linked to growing demands for transparency, ethical behaviour, and corporate social responsibility (CSR) from various stakeholders, including shareholders, consumers and industry organisations. It has also been identified as the secret superpower within us all to smash our goals like piñatas, if used correctly.[11]

In the meantime, let's get some much-needed clarity, and define the real meaning of accountability. According to the dictionary, 'accountability' means:

> *An individual's or organisation's obligation to account for its actions, accept responsibility for them and disclose the results in a transparent manner. It also includes financial or other entrusted property responsibilities.*

In everyday terms, accountability entails keeping promises or honouring commitments made to ourselves or others. There is a distinction to be made between accountability and responsibility; they are cousins rather than twins.

Allow me to explain.

We are **responsible** for things, and can only be **accountable** to people. Accountability entails keeping promises or honouring commitments made to ourselves or others.

Responsibility refers to the duties and obligations we have to complete tasks or achieve goals. It is the state of being in charge of something and is often linked to a specific role or position. For example, a project manager is responsible for ensuring that a project is completed on time and within budget.

Accountability, on the other hand, refers to the willingness to take responsibility for our actions and decisions. It is the act

---

11 I share game-changing accountability strategies in my book *The Accountability Advantage: Play your best game* that will help you realise your full potential and surpass your objectives using my 7-step Road to Accountability methodology. How exciting!

of answering for our actions, both to ourselves and to others. Accountability involves being answerable for the outcomes of our choices and decisions. For example, a project manager may be held accountable for the success or failure of a project.

Responsibility refers to the tasks or goals we are responsible for, while accountability refers to the consequences of our actions and decisions.

Responsibility *is about what we are tasked to do.*

Accountability *is about taking ownership of the results.*

It is through the power to say 'NO' that our commitments and beliefs are given life by accountability. The refusal of offers by saying 'NO' is a potent way for us to demonstrate how much we value accountability. It expresses our recognition that being accountable entails more than simply doing tasks; rather, it involves upholding the deeper expectations of our positions and the confidence that people have in us. By saying 'NO', we deliberately select the promises we can genuinely keep, making sure that our 'YES' speaks volumes about our commitment and moral character.

This discernment is essential because it enables us to handle our obligations in a way that is consistent with our values and talents, making us genuinely accountable for the results.

The refusal of offers by saying 'NO' allows us to infuse our commitments with integrity and intention, which is why I call it the 'oxygen of accountability'. It enables us to uphold a distinct line between accountability and responsibility, guaranteeing that we are actively involved in the process of keeping our word and acting honourably when we make commitments.

Saying 'NO' when it's required protects our capacity to keep our word and uphold our commitments – not just verbally but also in spirit – which highlights our dedication to responsibility. Therefore, learning to say 'NO' is a powerful confirmation of our commitment to accountability rather than a denial of it. It's an admission that even though we have a lot of responsibilities, we choose to hold ourselves accountable to our fundamental beliefs and the people we engage with.

As such, every 'YES' represents our commitment to excellence, and every 'NO' serves as a vital source of support for the accountability that upholds our moral standards and purpose.

The clarity that comes with 'NO'

Refusal of offers by saying 'NO' brings with it a great deal of clarity. Saying 'NO' results in a clarity that is freeing and essential for one's integrity and personal development. This clarity shows itself in several important spheres of our lives, transforming the way we engage with the outside world:

- ☒ **Saying 'NO' makes our priorities clear.** We speak about what really matters to us every time we decide not to accept anything that doesn't fit with our beliefs, objectives, or available resources. We can better focus our attention on the things that are truly essential.

- ☒ **Saying 'NO' helps to define limits in both our personal and professional interactions.** It defines the parameters of our interactions with others by letting them know what we are and aren't ready to tolerate. Since they guarantee respect and understanding for both parties, these boundaries are crucial for happy partnerships. We educate others on how to treat us when we are explicit about our boundaries, which results in interactions that are more thoughtful and kinder. In addition to safeguarding our wellbeing, this boundary clarity promotes partnerships built on sincere regard and concern.

- ☒ **Saying 'NO' helps us see ourselves more clearly.** It's a potent self-awareness activity that makes us continually evaluate and comprehend our limits, desires and capacities. Our sense of self is strengthened as a result of this introspection, which makes us more aware of our needs and self-assured in our capacity to speak out for ourselves. This gradually strengthens our sense of self-worth and self-respect as we recognise our freedom to make decisions that are best for us.

☒ **Saying 'NO' also demonstrates our dedication to our principles and objectives.** It is a proclamation that we will not be moved by outside forces or transient chances that do not advance our long-term goals. This perseverance is essential to realising our goals since it keeps us on course and prevents us from taking detours that aren't related to our main objectives.

Recognising the power of saying 'NO' empowers individuals to take charge of their lives, aligning daily decisions with long-term goals. This strategic refusal helps in managing time, energy, and resources effectively, ensuring focus on meaningful activities. By setting boundaries and resisting distractions, people can enhance their personal wellbeing, maintain mental clarity, and achieve a balanced, fulfilling life. Saying 'NO' also promotes ethical consumption, financial stability, and healthier habits, reinforcing autonomy and intentional living.

Top takeaways and lessons learned

- **Alignment with long-term goals:** Saying 'NO' enables alignment with long-term goals by preserving resources for meaningful activities, ensuring that your efforts are directed towards what truly matters to you.

- **Maintaining focus:** It helps maintain focus amid distractions, enhancing progress towards objectives by acting as a filter to keep your actions aligned with your priorities.

- **Supporting personal wellbeing:** Setting and respecting boundaries through 'NO' supports personal wellbeing and mental health, fostering mutual respect and understanding in your relationships.

- **Ethical consumption and financial stability:** Saying 'NO' fosters ethical consumption and financial stability by curbing impulsive spending and encouraging more deliberate, value-driven financial decisions.

- **Promoting health:** Rejecting unhealthy habits through 'NO' promotes physical and mental health, acting as a catalyst for positive change and long-term wellbeing.

- ☒ **Managing digital consumption:** Limiting digital consumption by saying 'NO' aids in maintaining mental clarity and deeper relationships, allowing for more meaningful and focused personal interactions.

- ☒ **Ensuring integrity and clear priorities:** Embracing 'NO' in relationships and accountability ensures integrity, clear priorities and mutual respect, helping you to stay true to your commitments and values.

Chapter 8

How to say 'NO': My 10-step framework

I t is crucial to provide a thoughtful response when saying 'NO' to an offer, and this is where my 10-step framework assists. The quality of our interactions and our shared respect are greatly impacted by how we communicate our boundaries in both personal and professional relationships. Relationship integrity is maintained when we communicate with respect and empathy, which demonstrates that even when we are voicing our demands, we also appreciate and comprehend the viewpoints of others. By reducing misconceptions and potential confrontations, this strategy promotes an environment of transparency and trust.

I frequently have to break down and role-play challenging conversations that team members have with their managers, as well as interactions that managers have with their teams, during my individual and group coaching sessions.

Saying 'NO' requires careful consideration. When we communicate with empathy and respect, we show that we not only understand and respect others' opinions but also appreciate and voice our own. This preserves the integrity of

If we all learned more suitable methods to say 'NO' in all aspects of our lives, we would all be more forthright and honest.

Darren Finkelstein

our relationships. By decreasing misunderstandings and the probability of confrontations, this tactic fosters a transparent and trustworthy atmosphere. The other person may get confused or resentful of abrupt and disrespectful refusals (saying 'NO') that lack explanation. We provide a thorough explanation to the other person to enable them to understand our perspective and the reasoning behind our decision. In addition to reducing unpleasant feelings, being honest and open with one another strengthens the bonds.

By role-playing these situations, managers and team members can practise stating 'NO' in a kind, understanding and straightforward way. Those lucky enough to be enrolled in my coaching program have found this to be of enormous value, as conversations can sometimes escalate, and the consequences of losing valued staff members and managers are significant. Those who practise these discussions can learn to create boundaries in a constructive way. It assists people in developing the skills necessary to handle difficult conversations with poise and assurance. This practice is crucial because it teaches people when and how to say 'NO' in social settings, which prevents misunderstandings and lays the groundwork for respect and understanding.

If we all learned more suitable methods to say 'NO' in all aspects of our lives, we would all be more forthright and honest. We can convey our boundaries with careful justifications that prevent unnecessary harm or misunderstanding. It ensures that people view our rejections as intentional decisions rather than arbitrary ones. This tactic creates a setting where people are at ease communicating their true wants and emotions, which leads to more sincere and meaningful interactions.

'Boundaries by Design'

In the bustling rhythm of modern life, where demands on our time and energy seem ever-expanding, the power of a consciously chosen 'NO' can be transformative. Enter 'Boundaries by Design', my meticulously crafted 10-step framework designed not just to empower you with the ability to say 'NO', but to elevate that choice into an art form that harmonises with your deepest values and priorities. This framework is not merely about declining requests or evading obligations; it's a blueprint for constructing a life of deliberate choice, free from the weight of unwelcome commitments and misaligned engagements.

At its core, 'Boundaries by Design' is born from the understanding that true fulfilment and balance stem from living in alignment with our core values. It's about recognising the fast-paced world of today, where demands on our time and energy seem to be increasing. Constantly learning to say 'NO' can have a profoundly positive impact. The 10-step structure presented in 'Boundaries by Design' is painstakingly created with the intention of not only giving you the confidence to say 'NO' but also to transform that decision into an expression that aligns with your core priorities and values.

'Boundaries by Design' is fundamentally based on the knowledge that leading a life that is consistent with our basic principles is the path to true fulfilment and equilibrium. This paradigm enables people to handle life's demands with grace, integrity and purpose by means of a deliberate examination of personal values, acknowledgement of boundaries, strategic assessment of requests, and clear and assertive communication.

Drawing on firsthand experiences, such as overcoming hardship and succeeding via calculated decision-making and strategic planning, 'Boundaries by Design' is more than just a technique; it's a monument to the transforming potential of defining and upholding one's own boundaries.

Accept the journey through 'Boundaries by Design' and learn how a life defined by choice rather than obligation can be unlocked by applying 'NO' with consideration. Let this book serve as your compass, guiding you towards a time when all of your commitments are a true representation of your values, all of your interactions have purpose, and your life is completely your own. Every 'YES' is a trade-off, an investment of our finite resources, and therefore, the judicious use of 'NO' becomes essential.

Through a thoughtful exploration of personal values, recognition of limits, strategic evaluation of requests, and clear, assertive communication, this framework empowers individuals to navigate life's demands with grace, integrity, and purpose.

Let's break down each step to ensure a comprehensive understanding and effective implementation.

'Boundaries by Design'

A 10-step framework for saying 'NO'

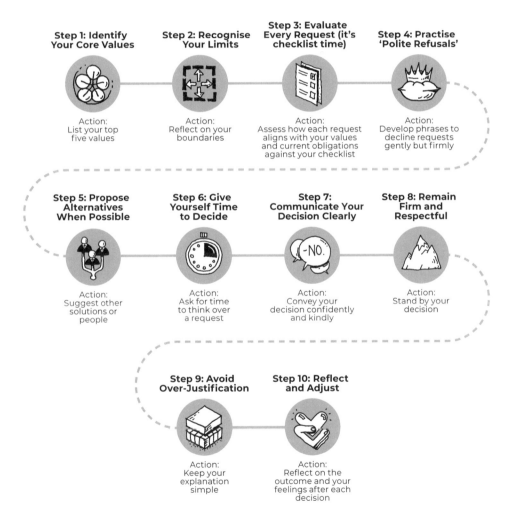

Step 1: Identify Your Core Values
Action:
List your top five values

Step 2: Recognise Your Limits
Action:
Reflect on your boundaries

Step 3: Evaluate Every Request (it's checklist time)
Action:
Assess how each request aligns with your values and current obligations against your checklist

Step 4: Practise 'Polite Refusals'
Action:
Develop phrases to decline requests gently but firmly

Step 5: Propose Alternatives When Possible
Action:
Suggest other solutions or people

Step 6: Give Yourself Time to Decide
Action:
Ask for time to think over a request

Step 7: Communicate Your Decision Clearly
Action:
Convey your decision confidently and kindly

Step 8: Remain Firm and Respectful
Action:
Stand by your decision

Step 9: Avoid Over-Justification
Action:
Keep your explanation simple

Step 10: Reflect and Adjust
Action:
Reflect on the outcome and your feelings after each decision

Step 1: Identify your core values

- ☒ **Action:** List your top five values.
- ☒ **Purpose:** To ensure your decisions align with what's most important to you.
- ☒ **Explanation:** Knowing your core values helps you navigate choices by acting as a compass.
- ☒ **Why:** Aligning actions with values leads to a more authentic and fulfilling life.

Top 5 implementation tips

1   Reflect on past decisions that felt right. What values were you honouring?
2   Consider moments of regret. Which values were compromised?
3   Use value-sort cards or lists to help identify and prioritise your values.
4   Revisit and adjust your values list periodically as you grow and evolve.
5   Share your core values with close friends or family for feedback and clarity.

Importance: Core values are the guiding principles of your life. Identifying these values helps you make choices that are in harmony with who you are and what you stand for, ensuring that your decisions, including the ability to say 'NO', align with your deepest convictions. This step serves as the foundation for the entire framework, as it ensures every decision you make is rooted in what's most important to you.

Step 2: Recognise your limits

- ☒ **Action:** Reflect on your boundaries.
- ☒ **Purpose:** To prevent over-commitment and burnout.
- ☒ **Explanation:** Understanding your limits in various aspects of life helps you set healthy boundaries.
- ☒ **Why:** Respecting your limits maintains your wellbeing and ensures you can commit fully to what you undertake.

Top 5 implementation tips

1 Regularly check in with yourself to assess your physical and emotional state.
2 Learn to recognise signs of fatigue and stress as indicators of your limits.
3 Communicate your boundaries clearly to others.
4 Practise self-care regularly to maintain your wellbeing.
5 Say 'NO' to minor things to practise enforcing your boundaries.

Importance: Recognising your limits is crucial to preventing overextension in your personal and professional lives. Understanding your physical, emotional and time constraints allows you to set realistic boundaries, protecting your wellbeing. This awareness ensures that when you commit, you can do so fully and effectively, reinforcing the importance of self-care and self-awareness.

Step 3: Evaluate every request (it's checklist time)

- ☒ **Action:** Assess how each request aligns with your values and current obligations against your checklist.
- ☒ **Purpose:** Ensures commitments are meaningful and manageable and fit in with those you deem important, which are identified in your checklist.
- ☒ **Explanation:** Each request should be considered in the context of your values, priorities and capacity.
- ☒ **Why:** This prioritisation ensures that you invest your time and energy in what's truly important.

Top 5 implementation tips

1 Create a criteria list to evaluate requests based on your values and priorities. This is your checklist.
2 Politely ask for time to think over a request before responding.
3 Consult with a mentor, trusted friend or your accountability coach if unsure about a request or the ramifications it may have in your organisation.
4 Keep a priority matrix or list to visualise where the request fits in.
5 Learn to discern between urgent and important requests.

Importance: This stage is essential for setting priorities and ensuring that your values and abilities are in line with the areas you choose as significant and that are listed on your checklist.

The checklist becomes a list of the items you think are crucial. If requests don't match, you should think about politely declining.

Here are some example checklists for personal and business applications.

Personal Checklist for Saying 'NO'

Based on the insights shared in my interview with Andrew Griffiths in chapter 6, here's a personal checklist to help you navigate when to say 'NO' and align your actions with your goals and values. This checklist is designed to facilitate thoughtful decision-making, ensuring that your commitments are purposeful and contribute to your personal and professional development.

☐ **Alignment with Goals**

- Does this opportunity align with my current personal and professional goals?
- How does this contribute to my long-term objectives?

☐ **Value Addition**

- Will saying 'YES' add value to my life or business?
- Does this opportunity resonate with my core values and principles?

☐ **Time and Resources**

- Do I have the necessary time and resources to commit to this without compromising my existing commitments?
- Will this opportunity require sacrifices, and are they worth it?

☐ **Personal Wellbeing**

- How will this impact my mental and physical wellbeing?
- Will engaging in this opportunity allow me to maintain a healthy work–life balance?

☐ **Opportunity Cost**

- What am I potentially giving up by saying 'YES' to this?
- Is the trade-off justified?

☐ **Brand and Integrity**

- Will this opportunity enhance or potentially harm my personal brand and integrity?
- How does this align with the reputation I wish to maintain or build?

☐ Need for Breathing Space

· Am I allowing myself time to thoroughly consider this opportunity?
· Have I created a buffer to think and assess without pressure?

☐ Learning from Role Models

· How would my mentors or role models handle this situation?
· Can I apply any of their approaches to saying 'NO' effectively and respectfully?

☐ Communication Strategy

· Have I considered how to communicate my refusal in a way that is respectful and maintains relationships?
· Can I articulate my reasons for saying 'NO' clearly and without feeling guilty?

☐ Openness to Future Opportunities

· Am I keeping the door open for future opportunities that may be a better fit?
· How can I decline in a way that keeps positive relations intact for potential collaboration down the line?

By going through this checklist whenever you're faced with a new opportunity or request, you can make more informed decisions that safeguard your time, align with your goals, and contribute to your overall wellbeing and success. Remember, saying 'NO' is not just about refusal; it's about making strategic choices that honour your priorities, values and vision for the future.

Use this QR code to download the personal checklist

Business Checklist for Saying 'NO'

Drawing from the interview with Andrew Griffiths in chapter 6, here's a business checklist to help you decide when to say 'NO' in a professional context. This checklist aims to ensure that your business decisions are strategic, reflective of your business goals, and conducive to growth and sustainability.

☐ **Strategic Alignment**
- Does this opportunity align with our business strategy and objectives for the current period?
- Will it drive us towards our long-term vision?

☐ **Brand Consistency**
- Is this opportunity consistent with our brand values and the message we want to convey to our audience?
- How might it impact our brand perception?

☐ **Resource Allocation**
- Do we have the necessary resources (time, finances, manpower) to commit to this without affecting our core operations?
- What would be the cost of diverting resources to this opportunity?

☐ **Return on Investment (ROI)**
- What is the potential return on investment, and does it justify the input?
- Are there clearer, more direct paths to achieving similar outcomes?

☐ **Opportunity Cost**
- By saying 'YES' to this, what other opportunities might we be missing out on?
- Is this the best use of our resources at this time?

☐ **Impact on Operations**
- Will this opportunity disrupt our current operations or workflow?
- Can we integrate this seamlessly, or will it require significant adjustments?

☐ Customer Impact

· How will this decision impact our customers or clients?
· Will it enhance their experience or potentially detract from it?

☐ Market Positioning

· Does this opportunity enhance our position in the market?
· Could it potentially open us up to unwanted competition or dilute our market presence?

☐ Learning from Past Decisions

· What have we learned from similar decisions in the past?
· Are there lessons from previous experiences that suggest saying 'NO' might be the best course of action?

☐ Communication and Negotiation

· How will we communicate our decision to stakeholders in a way that maintains or enhances relationships?
· Is there room for negotiation that could make the opportunity more aligned with our interests?

☐ Growth and Innovation

· Will this opportunity drive growth, innovation, or improvement within our business?
· Does it challenge us in a healthy way, or does it stretch us too thin?

☐ Ethical Considerations

· Are there any ethical concerns or potential conflicts of interest associated with this opportunity?
· Does it meet our standards for corporate social responsibility?

Use this QR code to download the business checklist

Step 4: Practise 'polite refusals'

- ☒ **Action:** Develop phrases to decline requests gently but firmly.
- ☒ **Purpose:** To say 'NO' without feeling guilty.
- ☒ **Explanation:** Having a repertoire of responses allows you to decline gracefully.
- ☒ **Why:** This minimises discomfort for both parties, making it easier to maintain relationships while respecting your boundaries.

Top 5 implementation tips

1 Practise your polite refusals with a friend or in front of a mirror.
2 Tailor your response to the situation for authenticity.
3 Keep a positive tone to soften the refusal.
4 Offer a brief reason, if appropriate, without over-explaining.
5 Remain consistent in your refusals to reinforce your boundaries.

Importance: Learning to say 'NO' in a manner that is both respectful and firm is key to maintaining healthy relationships and self-respect. This step emphasises the need for clear communication and the ability to decline requests without guilt or discomfort. It's a critical skill that enables you to stay true to your values and limits, highlighting the framework's commitment to assertive and compassionate communication.

Step 5: Propose alternatives when possible

- ☒ **Action:** Suggest other solutions or people.
- ☒ **Purpose:** To help within your capacity.
- ☒ **Explanation:** Offering alternatives shows your willingness to support, even if you can't fulfil the request yourself.
- ☒ **Why:** It maintains relationships and helps the requester achieve their goal.

Top 5 implementation tips

1. Keep a network list to refer requests to others who may help.
2. Offer resources or advice instead of direct assistance.
3. Set clear boundaries for what kind of help you can offer.
4. Ensure your suggestions are practical and helpful.
5. Follow up, if possible, to show genuine concern.

Importance: This step underlines the framework's principle of supportive networking and shows that declining a request doesn't mean shutting out opportunities for collaboration or assistance. It's about finding balance and fostering mutual respect and understanding.

Why not consider utilising the 5Ds that I outline in my book *The Accountability Advantage: Play your best game*? It's a specific strategy I've dubbed the '5Ds to Get Sh!t Done', aimed at increasing productivity and effectiveness in achieving goals. This is useful when searching for alternative ways to get a request completed without you having to take action, when saying 'NO' yields the best result for you. At least four out of these five would be suitable considerations in this step when you are looking for alternatives.

Here is a quick summary of each of the 5Ds:

1   **Do:** As the famous Nike tagline puts it, 'Just Do It' – there's no other way to go than to set aside the necessary time, bite the bullet, and finish the task at hand. Let's not give this much thought since, well, it won't help you say 'NO'.

2   **Delay:** It's acceptable to say 'NO' and provide a different timeline for when it works for you if you can't do the task, offer or request within the allotted time given to you by others. Never forget that your priorities are not the same priorities as those of others.

3   **Delegate:** Give someone else the task you are unable to complete. Someone else may be better suited to finish the task the required standard for a variety of reasons, such as the fact that they are more willing to take on more responsibility, or that this field better fits their KPI's or life's purpose. They could simply have more time available than you or could just be more engaged and interested in the task than you. Maybe they want to stretch themselves and take on more responsibilities to show others their desires, drive and capabilities.

4   **Delete:** Consider your stance, respectfully and empathetically answer 'NO', and be truthful about the reasons you give to demonstrate empathy and respect. Ahead in step 7, we will cover this in more detail.

5   **Call Darren:** In my experience, getting external support from someone who is essentially an outsider, detached from you emotionally and at arm's length, may be a terrific method to assess your priorities, align your priorities and provide a kick in the pants when necessary.

I'm happy to put my hand up; I have a lot of expertise and experience in this field. We'll talk about 'working with me' later in the book, and my contact information is there if you'd like to get in touch to better understand how my programs work for you individually or for your organisation.

Step 6: Give yourself time to decide

- ☒ **Action:** Ask for time to think over a request.
- ☒ **Purpose:** Prevents rash decisions.
- ☒ **Explanation:** Time allows for a thorough evaluation of how the request aligns with your priorities.
- ☒ **Why:** Ensures that your commitments are intentional and manageable.

Top 5 implementation tips

1 Develop a standard response for requesting time to decide.
2 Use the extra time to consult your priorities, checklist and schedule.
3 Set a specific timeframe for when you'll provide an answer.
4 Don't feel pressured to give an immediate response, even if pushed.
5 Use this time to practise saying 'NO' in your mind if leaning towards refusal.

Importance: This cautious approach ensures that you're not making commitments impulsively, reducing the likelihood of regret and overcommitment. It reinforces the framework's advocacy for thoughtful, deliberate decision-making.

Step 7: Communicate your decision clearly

- ☒ **Action:** Convey your decision confidently and kindly.
- ☒ **Purpose:** Ensures understanding and respect for your boundaries.
- ☒ **Explanation:** Clear communication prevents misunderstandings and respects both parties' expectations.
- ☒ **Why:** It's essential for maintaining healthy relationships and self-respect.

Top 5 implementation tips

1 Be direct and straightforward in your communication.
2 Maintain a calm and respectful tone.
3 Use 'I' statements to express your decision from your perspective.
4 Reinforce your decision if questioned, without getting defensive.
5 Acknowledge the other person's understanding and acceptance of your decision.

Importance: Clear communication about your decision prevents misunderstandings and sets the tone for how your boundaries are respected by others. This step is crucial for asserting your autonomy while still being respectful of others' needs and expectations. It embodies the framework's emphasis on clarity and assertiveness in interactions.

Step 8: Remain firm and respectful

- ☒ **Action:** Stand by your decision.
- ☒ **Purpose:** Demonstrates commitment to your boundaries.
- ☒ **Explanation:** Consistency in your decisions reinforces your boundaries.
- ☒ **Why:** It teaches others to respect your time and commitments.

Top 5 implementation tips

1 Remember your reasons for saying 'NO' if you start to waver.
2 Avoid getting drawn into negotiations over your decision.
3 Support your decision with your actions, not just words.
4 Stay calm and collected if your decision is challenged.
5 Reiterate your willingness to help in other ways, if possible.

Importance: Staying firm in your decision, even when faced with pressure, reinforces your commitment to your values and boundaries. This resilience is essential for establishing strong boundaries and ensuring they are respected. It illustrates the framework's principle of steadfastness in the face of external pressures, maintaining self-respect and integrity.

Step 9: Avoid over-justification

- ☒ **Action:** Keep your explanation simple.
- ☒ **Purpose:** Prevents weakening your position.
- ☒ **Explanation:** Over-explaining can lead to doubts and further persuasion attempts.
- ☒ **Why:** A simple, clear response is more powerful and less likely to be challenged.

Top 5 implementation tips

1 Plan your explanation in advance to keep it concise.
2 Focus on key points without elaborating on unnecessary details.
3 Practise assertiveness to convey your message confidently.
4 Politely decline further discussion on the matter if pressed.
5 Use non-verbal cues to reinforce your message, like firm body language.

Importance: Over-justification can undermine your decision and invite further debate. Keeping explanations simple and to the point respects both your own and the requester's time and mental space. This step highlights the framework's focus on maintaining boundaries without falling into defensive or over-explanatory modes, fostering a culture of respect and understanding.

Step 10: Reflect and adjust

- ☒ **Action:** Reflect on the outcome and your feelings after each decision.
- ☒ **Purpose:** Helps refine your approach to setting boundaries.
- ☒ **Explanation:** Self-reflection allows you to learn from each experience, improving your decision-making process.
- ☒ **Why:** Continuous improvement ensures your boundaries align with your evolving values and circumstances.

Top 5 implementation tips

1 Keep a journal of your reflections to track your progress.
2 Consider what went well and what could be improved.
3 Seek feedback from trusted individuals on your approach.
4 Adjust your strategies based on your reflections and feedback.
5 Celebrate your successes in maintaining your boundaries.

Importance: Reflection allows for personal growth and the continuous refinement of your boundary-setting skills. By evaluating the outcomes of your decisions and the processes leading to them, you can adjust your approach as needed, ensuring that your boundaries evolve with your changing values and circumstances. This step encapsulates the framework's dedication to lifelong learning and adaptability, emphasising the dynamic nature of personal growth and boundary setting.

Using the framework

Each step in 'Boundaries by Design' builds upon the previous ones, creating a comprehensive approach to setting and maintaining healthy boundaries. Starting from a foundation of self-understanding and moving towards active boundary management and reflective practices, the framework guides you through a process of intentional living. It emphasises the importance of being true to yourself, making conscious choices and navigating interpersonal dynamics with grace and assertiveness. Together, these steps form a holistic strategy for personal growth, relationship management and self-care, underpinning the framework's ultimate goal: to empower individuals to live authentically and purposefully, with a clear sense of their boundaries and a commitment to respecting them.

'Boundaries by Design' is a comprehensive guide to living with intention and purpose. By following these steps, you'll cultivate a life that respects your limits, honours your values, and enriches your relationships.

I invite you to download a copy of my personal and business checklists from my website. Remember to please modify the checklists to suit your own requirements and situation. My wish is that you can discover a procedure and approach that you find effective for your circumstances, as I have found mine to be.

Scan this QR code to download

The story behind the checklists

Within the fabric of life's struggles and triumphs, my narrative serves as a shining example of fortitude, astuteness and thoughtful decision-making. The foundation for this book, *NO: Building a life of choice without obligation*, and all four of my other business and boating books that I've written, published and sold worldwide are intricately woven with the threads of adversity, learning challenges and the triumph of spirit.

Throughout my experience, the checklists, a spreadsheet and well-considered plan have proven to be more than just a useful tool; they are an organised route through the maze of obstacles in life, especially for people juggling the intricacies of learning disabilities and social demands.

Overcoming adversity with structure

My story starts in the hallways of St George's Hospital in Kew, Victoria, Australia, where I was born, six-weeks premature – and in intensive care, hence I've never been late to anything since. It moves through the hardships of attending Vermont Primary School (1967–69), then the newly built Verdale Primary School (1969–72), and culminates at Doncaster High School (1973–79) at a critical juncture of difficulty and transformation.

The seeds of my resilience were sown there, in the midst of my unjust expulsion from Form 5 (year 11) after I embarrassingly repeated Form 4 (year 10), my battles with undiagnosed dyslexia, other comprehension issues, and the stigmatisation of both my Jewish heritage and my learning difficulties – which frequently resulted in beatings by bullies on my way home from school. Yep – they'd hide in bushes, and ambush me on my way home, carried out with military precision.

With all of this sometimes-traumatic background informa-tion and the lessons and teachings that were taken away from me by my expulsion from school, I have mostly survived and even thrived on my own self-taught processes, structures and frameworks that I have created out of necessity, as I chose to either fight or flee, otherwise I'd be overwhelmed.

For me, the basic 'checklist' became more than just an organising tool – it became a method for getting through obstacles. Every item that was crossed off the list was much more than simply a chore or assignment; it represented a victory over my learning impairments and the scars left by early discrimination and antisemitism. It also represented a departure from my personal beliefs, predetermined standards and ideals.

A checklist gives me a set of checks and balances to ensure that when I'm making a decision, I'm doing it in my own time and not someone else's. I can also do this without emotional connections or ties, giving me back the control to assess any request, give an answer that is right for me, and say 'YES' or 'NO'.

Quite often I choose to say 'NO' as this gives me the much-needed time and space I need to determine what's right for me given the circumstances.

Strategic planning as a path to success

My basic checklist changed as I entered the corporate world and when I met and worked alongside Steve Jobs and other Apple greats, such former CEO Dr Gil Amelio, design guru Sir Jony Ive, and marketing whiz Phil Schiller, while working for 10 amazing years as Manager of Commercial Markets in Australia. Next, I started my own lifestyle company in the marine sector, which I sold with my business partner Andrew Rose before successfully exiting after 15 years together. I managed to fit in eight years as the resident Beach 'N' Bay reporter for Melbourne's top radio station, 3AW, where I would do over a hundred live crosses every summer.

My go-to tool for manoeuvring through the complexities and unknowns of the business world was the humble checklist. My ability to deploy my special strengths – resilience, strategic thinking and unwavering determination to succeed – came from my thorough dissection of difficult undertakings and decisions into small, actionable pieces. Like eating an elephant, one piece at a time.

My strategic execution relied heavily on checklists, spreadsheets and solid plans to achieve my goals, which helped me decide carefully and intelligently when to say 'YES' or 'NO'. It was not merely a component of my planning process.

The power of deliberate choice

Making time for thoughtful, deliberate decision-making is maybe the most important lesson to be learned from my experience. I developed the capacity to stop, think and make deliberate decisions using my checklists.

Whether in my personal or business life, this practice made sure that every decision I made was deliberate and in line with my beliefs, aspirations, goals and the life I imagined for myself, rather than just a reflexive response to outside forces, or someone else's priorities.

I have been able to live a life of choice without obligation because of my methodical approach to decision-making, which is supported and underpinned by the modest checklist.

Empowering others through shared wisdom

By offering my personal and professional checklists to my readers, I am helping others who are struggling with their own issues. This sharing is an invitation to accept a disciplined approach to life's decisions and challenges, going beyond simple altruism.

My checklists provide not only useful advice but also encouragement and hope, showing that it is possible to get through even the worst situations in life if you have the correct resources and attitude.

The narrative I present in this book is proof that checklists work.

The bedrock of making empowered and strategic decisions, both in our personal lives and in the business realm, lies in the collection of good and accurate data, hence my love for checklists, spreadsheets and well-documented plans. Where was all that important stuff back in my old Computer Office Supplies days?

Isn't hindsight a wonderful thing?

Nothing beats accurate data

In a world inundated with information, discerning the valuable from the trivial becomes paramount, providing us with insights necessary to navigate the complexities of life and commerce.

Particularly when adopting the principle of saying 'NO' to build a life of choice without obligation, the clarity that comes from well-analysed data is indispensable.

It equips us with the confidence to refuse what doesn't align with our core values and goals, ensuring that our commitments are deliberate and meaningful.

Accurate data acts as a compass, guiding us through the fog of daily demands and opportunities, allowing us to make informed choices that reflect our priorities and lead to a more fulfilled and balanced existence. In essence, the foundation of informed decision-making – whether to pursue an opportunity and say 'YES' or to decline it and say 'NO' – rests on the integrity and relevance of the data we base our choices on.

By sharing my experiences, I wish to inspire others by demonstrating that a life of happiness, success and genuine freedom can be crafted with planning, strategy and thoughtful decision-making.

CHAPTER 8 REVIEW

'Boundaries by Design' is a 10-step framework that empowers individuals to say 'NO' effectively and intentionally. This framework emphasises aligning decisions with core values and personal goals, maintaining healthy boundaries, and enhancing communication skills to foster mutual respect and understanding. By providing practical steps and implementation tips, the chapter guides readers through the process of evaluating requests, practising polite refusals, proposing alternatives, and reflecting on outcomes. The framework is rooted in personal experiences and aims to help readers live authentically, purposefully and free from unwelcome commitments.

Top takeaways and lessons learned

- ☒ **Identify core values:** Determine your top five values to ensure decisions align with what matters most to you.

- ☒ **Recognise your limits:** Reflect on your physical, emotional and time constraints to set realistic boundaries and prevent burnout.

- ☒ **Evaluate every request:** Assess how each request aligns with your priorities and obligations, using a personal checklist for guidance.

- ☒ **Practise polite refusals:** Develop phrases to decline requests gently but firmly, maintaining respect and clarity in your communication.

- ☒ **Propose alternatives:** Suggest other solutions or people who might help, showing willingness to support within your capacity.

- ☒ **Give yourself time to decide:** Ask for time to think over requests to make thoughtful, intentional commitments.

- ☒ **Reflect and adjust:** Regularly evaluate the outcomes of your decisions and refine your approach to setting boundaries for continuous improvement.

Chapter 9

101 reasons why saying 'NO' is so effective

I've created a comprehensive list of my 101 reasons why saying 'NO' is effective, and I've not bitten the bullet to rank those most important #1 to my personal choice of #101, my least important, which I'm leaving for you to do.

Having a comprehensive list of 101 reasons why saying 'NO' is effective serves as a powerful tool for personal empowerment and clarity. This extensive collection reflects the myriad facets of life where the power of refusal can bring about profound positive changes.

One of the key benefits of having 101 reasons to choose from is the flexibility it offers. Life is complex and varied, and the situations that call for a firm 'NO' are equally diverse. With such a comprehensive list, you can find a reason that resonates with your specific circumstance at any given moment. This ensures that your decision to say 'NO' is backed by a solid understanding and justification, enhancing your confidence and resolve. Moreover, this extensive list validates the wide range of emotions and scenarios people experience, making the concept of refusal accessible and relatable to a broader audience.

Additionally, the process of compiling and reflecting on 101 reasons underscores the significance of intentionality in decision-making. It encourages a deeper examination of your values, priorities and boundaries. By engaging with this extensive list, you cultivate a more profound self-awareness and a stronger sense of agency. It transforms the act of saying 'NO' from a potentially negative or guilt-ridden response into a positive affirmation of self-respect and personal choice.

Furthermore, this list serves as an educational and inspirational resource. If you struggle with the notion of refusal or feel pressured to conform to others' demands, the list offers a wealth of insights and perspectives. It demonstrates that saying 'NO' is not only acceptable but also beneficial in numerous ways. By illustrating the many positive outcomes of asserting boundaries, you empower others to embrace their right to say 'NO' and to do so with conviction and grace.

In essence, having 101 reasons why saying 'NO' is effective provides a comprehensive framework for understanding and embracing the power of refusal. It highlights the importance of personal choice, respects individual boundaries, and promotes a healthier, more intentional approach to life's demands.

This extensive list is more than a compilation of reasons; it is a manifesto for living a life of choice without obligation.

Here's my attempt to curate such a list, recognising that the importance of each reason can vary greatly depending on individual circumstances and values.

1 **Preserves personal boundaries:** Ensures your personal limits are respected.

2 **Reduces stress:** Avoids overcommitment, which can lead to stress.

3 **Promotes self-respect:** Shows self-worth by not always acquiescing to others' demands.

4 **Encourages self-care:** Allows time for your own needs and health.

5 **Improves time management:** Frees up time for what truly matters to you.

6   **Protects from exploitation:** Prevents others from taking advantage of your kindness or efforts.

7   **Enhances decision-making:** Encourages thoughtful choices rather than automatic 'YESes'.

8   **Fosters independence:** Shows you can stand firm in your decisions.

9   **Prioritises personal goals:** Helps you focus on achieving your own objectives.

10 **Boosts confidence:** Builds the courage to express your true feelings and opinions.

11 **Cultivates authentic relationships:** Attracts people who respect your choices.

12 **Encourages mutual respect:** Demonstrates that respect is a two-way street.

13 **Improves quality of work:** Allows you to dedicate effort to fewer tasks, enhancing quality.

14 **Reduces resentment:** Prevents feelings of being taken for granted or used.

15 **Promotes honest communication:** Encourages open and honest dialogues.

16 **Prevents burnout:** Reduces the risk of mental, emotional and physical exhaustion.

17 **Enhances creativity:** Frees up mental space for creative thinking.

18 **Maintains physical health:** Avoids stress-related health issues by not overextending yourself.

19 **Encourages self-exploration:** Gives you space to understand your likes, dislikes and limits.

20 **Builds professional respect:** Demonstrates that your time and expertise are valuable.

21 **Supports work–life balance:** Ensures personal time is not always sacrificed for work.

22 **Teaches others to value you:** Shows that your contributions and time are precious.

23 **Promotes personal growth:** Challenges you to step out of your comfort zone when necessary.

24 **Improves mental health:** Decreases anxiety and depression risk by avoiding overwhelming situations.

25 **Encourages responsibility:** Teaches others to be responsible for their own needs and wants.

26 **Fosters a sense of empowerment:** Feeling in control of your life choices boosts empowerment.

27 **Promotes clear priorities:** Helps distinguish between what's urgent and what's important.

28 **Encourages problem-solving:** Forces others to find solutions rather than relying on you.

29 **Safeguards personal interests:** Ensures your hobbies and interests are not sidelined.

30 **Encourages respect for your time:** Signals that your time is valuable and shouldn't be wasted.

31 **Facilitates better relationships:** By saying 'NO' to others, you can say 'YES' to closer family and friends.

32 **Promotes financial health:** Prevents spending on things that don't align with your financial goals.

33 **Encourages others' independence:** Helps others learn to do things for themselves.

34 **Supports emotional wellbeing:** Avoids emotional drain from too many commitments.

35 **Enhances focus:** Allows for deeper focus on fewer tasks or relationships.

36 **Promotes a sense of peace:** Less cluttered schedule means a more peaceful mind.

37 **Encourages personal integrity:** Stay true to your beliefs and values.

38 **Facilitates leadership skills:** Demonstrates the ability to make tough decisions.

39 **Improves negotiation skills:** Often a 'NO' can lead to a better compromise.

40 **Builds assertiveness:** Develops the ability to state your needs and desires clearly.

41 **Reduces clutter:** Both in physical spaces (by refusing things) and in your schedule.

42 **Promotes a sense of control:** Over your life and the direction it's taking.

43 **Encourages flexibility:** Saying 'NO' to one thing can mean saying 'YES' to unexpected opportunities.

44 **Facilitates personal satisfaction:** Doing what you love or believe in leads to personal fulfillment.

45 **Encourages realistic self-assessment:** Recognising your limits is a sign of self-awareness.

46 **Supports effective delegation:** Encourages finding the right person for a task, not just you.

47 **Encourages innovation:** Saying 'NO' to the status quo can inspire new ways of thinking.

48 **Builds patience:** For yourself and others, as you seek out the best decisions.

49 **Promotes self-reliance:** Demonstrates your ability to stand up for yourself.

50 **Facilitates mindfulness:** Promotes being present and making conscious decisions.

51 **Encourages life balance:** Helps maintain a balance among various aspects of life.

52 **Supports goal achievement:** By not getting sidetracked by others' demands.

53 **Promotes risk management:** Avoids potential pitfalls by not overcommitting.

54 **Encourages learning to let go:** Not everything needs your attention or effort.

55 **Builds resilience:** The ability to say 'NO' strengthens emotional resilience.

56 **Encourages appreciation of time alone:** Valuing solitude for reflection and rest.

57 **Promotes strategic thinking:** Planning your 'YESes' and 'NOs' with purpose and foresight.

58 **Facilitates joy in doing less:** Finding happiness in simplicity and not overdoing.

59 **Encourages efficient use of resources:** Time, energy and money are used more wisely.

60 **Supports personal convictions:** Standing firm in your beliefs despite external pressures.

61 **Promotes personal safety:** Saying 'NO' to risky or harmful situations.

62 **Encourages ethical behaviour:** Avoiding actions that conflict with your moral compass.

63 **Facilitates environmental stewardship:** Saying 'NO' to wasteful practices.

64 **Promotes sustainable living:** By refusing what you don't need or what harms the environment.

65 **Encourages community engagement:** Focusing on what benefits your community.

66 **Facilitates global awareness:** Saying 'NO' to things that harm the global community.

67 **Encourages cultural appreciation:** Focusing on meaningful cultural experiences.

68 **Supports diversity and inclusion:** Making space for diverse voices and experiences.

69 **Encourages historical awareness:** Learning from the past to make informed decisions.

70 **Facilitates artistic expression:** More time for creative pursuits.

71 **Encourages scientific exploration:** Time to pursue interests in science and innovation.

72 **Supports educational goals:** Focusing on learning and personal development.

73 **Promotes physical fitness:** More time for exercise and health.

74 **Encourages nutritional health:** Time to focus on eating well.

75 **Supports mental clarity:** Less clutter, more clear thinking.

76 **Encourages spiritual growth:** Time for reflection and spiritual practices.

77 **Promotes emotional intelligence:** Understanding and managing your emotions better.

78 **Facilitates conflict resolution:** Learning to handle disagreements positively.

79 **Encourages creative problem-solving:** Finding unique solutions to challenges.

80 **Supports effective communication:** Clear and concise expression of thoughts and needs.

81 **Encourages diplomacy:** Handling situations with tact and consideration.

82 **Facilitates cultural sensitivity:** Being mindful of cultural differences in interactions.

83 **Promotes global citizenship:** Recognising your part in the larger world.

84 **Encourages environmental conservation:** Making choices that protect the environment.

85 **Supports social justice:** Standing up for fairness and equity.

86 **Encourages historical preservation:** Valuing and preserving heritage and history.

87 **Facilitates community service:** Dedication to helping and serving others.

88 **Encourages lifelong learning:** The pursuit of knowledge and skills.

89 **Promotes personal enlightenment:** Achieving a higher state of awareness or understanding.

90 **Supports global health:** Making decisions that benefit the health of the global community.

91 **Encourages technological innovation:** Embracing new technologies for a better future.

92 **Supports sustainable development:** Commitment to responsible growth and development.

93 **Encourages economic stability:** Making financially responsible decisions.

94 **Supports animal welfare:** Making choices that consider the wellbeing of animals.

95 **Encourages ethical consumption:** Choosing products and services responsibly.

96 **Supports renewable energy:** Advocating for and using sustainable energy sources.

97 **Encourages conservation of resources:** Efficient and responsible use of natural resources.

98 **Supports biodiversity:** Protecting and valuing the variety of life.

99 **Encourages cultural diversity:** Valuing and engaging with diverse cultural expressions.

100 **Supports peace and security:** Making decisions that contribute to a peaceful existence.

101 **Encourages global understanding:** Fostering an understanding and appreciation of global interconnectivity.

Each reason emphasises the power and importance of saying 'NO' in various facets of life, underscoring the significance of choice, personal agency and the impact of our decisions on ourselves and the world around us.

Why don't you write your own list, and have a go at ranking them?

CHAPTER 9 REVIEW

Having a comprehensive list of 101 reasons why saying 'NO' is effective serves as a powerful tool for personal empowerment and clarity. This extensive collection reflects the myriad facets of life where the power of refusal can bring about profound positive changes. With such a comprehensive list, you can find a reason that resonates with your specific circumstance at any given moment. This ensures that your decision to say 'NO' is backed by a solid understanding and justification, enhancing your confidence and resolve. Additionally, the process of compiling and reflecting on these reasons encourages a deeper examination of your values, priorities and boundaries, transforming the act of saying 'NO' into a positive affirmation of self-respect and personal choice. The list serves as both an educational and inspirational resource, empowering you to embrace your right to say 'NO' with conviction and grace. Ultimately, this collection highlights the importance of personal choice, respects individual boundaries, and promotes a healthier, more intentional approach to life's demands.

Top takeaways and lessons learned

- ☒ **Empowerment and clarity:** Saying 'NO' is a powerful tool for personal empowerment and clarity, helping you set and respect your boundaries.

- ☒ **Flexibility:** A comprehensive list offers flexibility to find reasons that resonate with specific circumstances, enhancing your confidence.

- ☒ **Intentional decision-making:** Reflecting on these reasons encourages a deeper examination of values, priorities and boundaries.

- ☒ **Positive affirmation:** Transforms saying 'NO' into a positive affirmation of self-respect and personal choice.

- ☒ **Educational resource:** Serves as an educational tool for those struggling with refusal, offering insights and perspectives.

☒ **Inspirational resource:** Demonstrates the benefits of asserting boundaries, empowering you to say 'NO' with conviction.

☒ **Promotes healthier living:** Highlights the importance of personal choice and respects individual boundaries, promoting a more intentional approach to life's demands.

Let's bring it all together ...

Final thoughts

Having a voice consistent with your own objectives, aspirations, purpose and reason (your why) is essential to living your life authentically. It shapes more than just who you are. Instead of using 'NO' as a negative response, this alignment enables you to use it as an affirmative action that protects your life's purpose. Being able to decline opportunities or requests when they present themselves without feeling guilty comes from having a firm understanding of your priorities. Instead of being a barrier to progress, this denial, your 'NO', is a strategic move that ensures you continue on your chosen course.

Saying 'NO' to attractive offers that don't fit with your passion, for example, will help you stay loyal to your professional trajectory if your goal is to build a career in an area you're enthusiastic about.

Saying 'NO' frees you from a web of commitments that don't align with your overall goals. It functions as a shield to protect the integrity of your time, focus and energy, so that you can devote them solely to activities that advance your objectives. Saying 'NO' to after-work events, for example, allows you to dedicate your nights to the online course that will help you get closer to your ideal career. This refusal-based self-guardianship is about keeping the path open for the journey you have planned, not about blocking off paths.

Saying 'NO' is an art, but it must be matched with the calculated wisdom of saying 'YES'. Sometimes, affirmative action, a good ole 'YES', is the key to win–win situations, the path to personal development, or just the right thing to do at the time.

Saying 'YES' could result from realising that making a brief sacrifice can have long-term advantages, such as accepting a short-term project that will test your limits but greatly expand your skillset and give you a much-needed 'stretch' when you are feeling way too comfortable.

There will be instances all through our lives where 'YES' is required by the roles we do, such as a project that is under your job description, a duty to assist a close friend in need, or a commitment to a family member, especially if they are from the older generation, where it's too difficult to explain why not and easier to just do it.

These responsibilities are the threads that, when carefully woven, can enhance the fabric of our lives; they are not incompatible with the pursuit of a life of choice.

Expressing 'YES' when it's appropriate and why is just as much an expression of your agency as expressing 'NO'. It's about deciding which obligations fit into your larger life plan and are consistent with your ideals. For instance, even if it means stepping outside of your present comfort zone and into a role that better fits your professional goals, you can say 'YES' to taking on more responsibility at work. Naturally, the role should fit into your bigger purpose and your why.

Saying 'YES' while your inner voice says 'NO' is normal, acceptable, healthy and sometimes even required. This frequently entails putting longer-term factors ahead of short-term choices. One important factor is that the best course of action at any given time may necessitate giving in or making a sacrifice for the sake of the greater good, which might include your own development, the success of a group project, the long-term game, your bigger picture, or to benefit an important relationship.

In both the personal and business spheres, saying 'YES' could strategically lead to benefits down the road or avert setbacks. A professional might, for instance, consent to taking on an additional task if they believe it would help them grow in their career or if they believe that refusing it will lower their status or reputation within the organisation. Similar to this, even if our natural reaction would be to say 'NO', we could agree to help a family member move house or attend an event out of respect

Discover freedom of choice.
Start with 'NO'.

Darren Finkelstein

for a connection. These 'YESes' are admissions that our acts frequently have a ripple effect outside of our personal spheres.

There are times when power demands submission. Following a request from management in the workplace can be seen as an acceptance of the roles and hierarchies that support organisational function, even if your first response is resistance. Saying 'YES' to a parent's request might be seen in personal dynamics as a sign of appreciation or duty, or to show respect to one's elders.

Of course, let's not forget the charitable component. Saying 'YES' to assist someone in need can be a sign of compassion, generosity and conscience. In these situations, what we do is a reflection of a larger ethical position that respects other people's wellbeing and our place in the social structure.

In many cases, saying 'YES' becomes a nuanced choice that, although it conflicts with the initial desire to say 'NO', is in line with a longer-term goal, respect for authority or a dedication to other people's welfare. These choices frequently call for a careful balancing act between judgement, vision and selflessness. They serve as a reminder that the decisions we make affect not just our own course but also the lives and systems of which we are a part. Saying 'YES' in these situations is wise because it acknowledges that our personal preferences are only one element of the intricate web of relationships and obligations that mould our lives.

Saying 'NO' basically means having the guts and the insight to accept what you do want, rather than just turning down what you don't want.

This allows you to live a life of freedom and responsibility. Every 'YES' and 'NO' you choose to make is a brushstroke in the painting of your life, where the colours you choose to apply to the canvas represent the shades of your truest self.

Your personal and professional life will be shaped by your profound comprehension of these concepts, which will also affect the level of fulfillment you experience as you make complex life decisions.

Master list: Condensing essential takeaways

A thorough fact sheet that condenses the most important advice and highlights from the art of saying 'NO' can be obtained by creating a master list from the abundance of insights gained throughout the chapters of this book. With the help of this list, you can create a life of choice, accomplishment and balance, while upholding civil and wholesome relationships.

20 essential tips for saying 'NO':

1   **Self-determination through 'NO':** Acknowledge that stating 'NO' can empower you to make decisions that are strategically aligned with your values and objectives.

2   **Dispel the negativity myth:** Recognise that, when applied carefully, saying 'NO' can actually have good effects rather than just being a negative word.

3   **Allocating strategic resources:** Say 'NO' to better manage time and energy and concentrate on things that are important.

4   **Sustain healthy relationships:** To promote mutual respect and understanding in relationships, strike a balance between expressing 'NO' and being clear and empathetic.

5   **Abandon shame, accept self-respect:** See 'NO' as an act of self-decency and establish boundaries instead of carrying the shame connected with it.

6   **Assertiveness in professional integrity:** Showcase your leadership abilities by learning to say 'NO' when it comes to setting priorities and handling workload in a professional setting.

7   **Practice and habituation:** With consistent practice, you can become more adept at saying 'NO', which will eventually become simpler and more instinctive.

8   **Cultural and historical sensitivity:** Be mindful of the many historical and cultural viewpoints on rejection and modify your strategy accordingly.

9   **Establishing and communicating clear personal boundaries:** This is essential for maintaining emotional stability and positive interpersonal dynamics.

10 **Self-awareness for effective communication:** Identify your own requirements and constraints so that you may honestly explain your rejection.

11 **Strike a balance between assertiveness and sensitivity:** Understand the consequences of saying 'NO' while remaining steadfast in your demands.

12 **Freedom from obligation:** Live a life in which decisions are made voluntarily, for your own satisfaction, rather than as a requirement.

13 **Determine and align with long-term goals:** Say 'NO' to distractions and obligations that are not in line with your long-term goals.

14 **Create digital boundaries:** Clearly define the boundaries around the usage of technology to preserve mental space and encourage meaningful interactions.

15 **Accept discomfort for growth:** Push yourself past your comfort zone to strengthen your fortitude and accept fresh chances for introspection.

16 **Handle relationships carefully:** When establishing limits, be aware of how they will affect other people's feelings and communicate openly.

17 **Learn 'NO' to accept accountability:** Consider saying 'NO' as a proclamation of your dedication to your moral principles and integrity – making decisions deliberately.

18 **Engage in mindful consumption:** Say 'NO' to impulsive purchases, pointless outlays and unsustainable consumption habits.

19 **Develop courage against social norms:** Refuse to conform to social norms and use the word 'NO' to uphold your own ideals and goals.

20 **Respectfully express your thoughts, feelings and beliefs:** By saying 'NO' in a courteous, concise and thoughtful manner, you can maintain connections and promote understanding among others.

Don't forget my 10-step framework

The core of saying 'NO' as an empowering tool for creating a life of choice, balance and fulfilment is encapsulated in my 10-step framework 'Boundaries by Design'. Don't forget to download my important checklists, for personal and business use, to help you set your own decision-making criteria. I'd love to see you follow these recommendations and handle your personal and business lives with integrity, focus and a deep sense of success. You can also maintain respectful and harmonious relationships.

We have submerged ourselves in great detail on the nuanced meaning of saying 'NO'. We've unravelled the social, historical and cultural nuances that shape our understanding and application of this powerful term by examining the sense of personal strength and autonomy that can be achieved through deliberate rejection. Saying 'NO' is a deliberate choice that highlights our goals, limits and principles in both our personal and professional lives. It's not just a reflex. This theme appears through all the chapters. It is proof of your affirmation of your individuality and your upholding of your moral principles in the face of external obligations.

Saying 'NO' when necessary is an essential ability for preserving harmony, creating positive dynamics and guaranteeing respect in both personal and professional contexts. You can negotiate the intricacies of interpersonal relationships with elegance and authenticity by being forceful and empathetic, which eventually results in more satisfying partnerships. This book also emphasises the necessity of introspection and self-awareness in recognising your own boundaries and principles, which helps you communicate more effectively and make deliberate judgements.

Examining the many cultural and historical viewpoints on refusal sheds light on the various ways in which societies have managed to strike a balance between social cohesion and individual liberty. This context highlights the significance of cultural sensitivity and tact in its use and deepens our knowledge of 'NO' as a nuanced expression formed by religious, cultural and societal influences.

It's not what you say,
it's the way you say it.

Don Finkelstein (1930–2022)

'NO' is emphasised as a fundamental pillar for emotional wellbeing and mental health throughout the chapters, which also emphasise personal boundaries and self-care. You can protect your time, energy and emotional reserves by setting and adhering to personal boundaries, which promotes a more balanced and satisfying existence. Furthermore, the deliberate application of 'NO' to align with long-term objectives and aspirations emphasises the tool's importance for both professional and personal development by helping you concentrate your energies on what really counts.

The need to set technological boundaries and use discretion when consuming digital content in the digital era tackles the problems of digital distractions and information overload. Regaining your time and attention, developing closer bonds with others, and maintaining your online safety all depend on following these guidelines.

'NO' is a liberating force that allows you to live a life of choice, free from excessive duty and in line with your innermost goals and values. It is an exhortation to live purposefully and to embrace the transformational potential of refusal, and to foster an environment of respect and accountability.

You can lay the groundwork for true fulfilment and content-ment by incorporating the teachings from each chapter into your life, giving you more clarity, purpose and autonomy.

Good luck with your decision-making, and remember my dear old dad's advice:

Onward to the goldfields.

THE ACCOUNTABILITY GUY ®

WORK WITH ME

What's next?

That is a very good question ...

Well, well, well, congratulations! You have now reached the end of this book. I hope you have found the journey as enlightening and empowering as I intended. Throughout these pages, we have explored the transformative power of saying 'NO' and how it can help you build a life of choice without obligation. My goal has been to offer you a pathway to greater freedom and liberation, helping you to prioritise your goals, dreams and desires.

If the concepts and strategies discussed in this book resonate with you, and you find yourself inspired by the idea of living a life defined by your own choices, I encourage you to consider taking the next step with me. Working together, we can delve deeper into these principles and tailor them specifically to your unique situation. Whether you are looking to enhance your personal life, elevate your professional career, or simply gain more control over your daily decisions, my expertise can guide you in making those powerful 'NOs' that pave the way to your true aspirations.

Thank you for joining me on this journey. It has been a privilege to share these insights with you, and I hope they have sparked a sense of empowerment and clarity in your life.

Remember, the ability to say 'NO' is not just about refusing what doesn't serve you; it's about creating space for what truly matters. If you're ready to take the next step towards a more intentional and fulfilling life, I would be honoured to work with you and support you in achieving your dreams.

As the author of this book, and The Accountability Guy®, my mission is to help high-performing entrepreneurs, business owners, managers, their teams and individuals like you achieve more than you ever thought possible.

With a wealth of experience and a track record of success, I understand the unique challenges faced by ambitious individuals striving to reach the next level. If you are working hard but still struggling to achieve your goals, feeling overwhelmed by the demands of your business, or needing direction to elevate your enterprise, then you have come to the right place.

Here are four compelling reasons why you need to work with me:

1   You're working hard, but you're still not achieving your goals.

2   You feel so overwhelmed that it's genuinely overwhelming.

3   You need direction on how to get your business or organisation to the next stage.

4   You're a high-performer and successful, but you wish to juggle even more balls in the air to be more successful.

Accountability coaching is not about punishing those who lack the desire to succeed. It's quite the opposite. It's about providing the support, direction and motivation necessary to help you smash your goals with the force of a cricket bat or baseball bat hitting a piñata.

My approach is all about **G**etting **S**h*t **D**one (GSD) and ensuring you have the clarity and focus needed to achieve your dreams by removing those energy-zapping, time-wasting and off-piste distractions.

The time has come to act. If you're ready to take your life and business to new heights, let's work together to make it happen. Embrace the power of 'NO' and build the life of choice you deserve.

Thank you for joining me on this journey, and I look forward to the incredible achievements we can accomplish together.

Explore the following list of options and choices that you might choose from as you proceed.

Self-reflection

Think back on the main lessons you learned from the chapters.

- ☒ Determine the areas of your life – both personal and professional – where you could attain balance, focus and accomplishment by learning to say 'NO'.

- ☒ Think about how accepting 'NO' could help with issues like idea overload, procrastination paralysis and decision-making hesitation.

Visit my website

Here, you will find resources and insights geared towards empowering entrepreneurs, business owners, teams and individuals to turn their ideas into reality.

This platform serves as a beacon for those seeking to enhance their accountability and execution capabilities.

Discover your Accountability Score and increase the probability of smashing your GOALS and Getting Sh!t Done!

Why take the quiz?

(In case smashing your goals like piñatas with a cricket bat isn't enough!)

- ☒ Answer 26 yes/no questions in under 4 minutes.
- ☒ Get a personalised report, tailored to you, with clear action steps.
- ☒ It's totally FREE – $0.
- ☒ Accountability is a superpower.

Take the free Accountability Assessment

- ☒ **Procrastination paralysis?**
- ☒ **Ideas overload**
- ☒ **Remove distractions; say 'NO'**

Boost your execution with my 15-minute Accountability Assessment

Engage with my complimentary 15-minute Accountability Assessment with Darren Finkelstein (that's me) over Zoom.

This no-strings-attached evaluation is designed to provide a quick but insightful analysis of your current accountability levels and identify key areas for improvement.

Identify your challenges

During the assessment, focus on pinpointing the ONE thing that is significantly hindering your capacity to get things done.

This could be a recurring bottleneck in your decision-making process, a tendency towards procrastination, or the overwhelming influx of ideas without a clear strategy for implementation.

Book into a Coaching Program

This is my signature series of individual and group coaching programs for business owners, C-suite executives, entrepreneurs, managers and your teams.

You can meet weekly, fortnightly or monthly directly with me and together we'll lift your output, so you can smash your goals like piñatas with cricket and/or baseball bats.

- ☒ **GET CLARITY** – so you know what to do FIRST
- ☒ **GET STARTED** – so you know what to do NEXT
- ☒ **GET STUFF DONE** – so you know what to do MORE of

Does this sound familiar...?

- ☒ You're trying to juggle more balls in order to become even more successful.
- ☒ You're working hard but find it difficult to direct your attention and energy in the right direction.
- ☒ You feel so overwhelmed that you end up procrastinating because you don't know what the first step is.
- ☒ You need some direction on what to do next to take your business to the next level.
- ☒ Your To-Do Lists (or timeboxes) are getting longer instead of getting To-Done.
- ☒ You're missing deadlines, breaking promises and letting yourself and others down.

It's time to start taking action before people realise you're full of it ...

Engage Darren as your guest speaker for your next event, conference or workshop

I'm known to be an engaging professional speaker and presenter who will compel your audience and participants to take action.

Request that I speak at your next conference, webinar, event or workshop, either live in person or virtually over Zoom (or similar).

Let's talk about your upcoming events, conferences, workshops or offsites, and how I can help you bring the game-changing topic of 'Accountability' to the table.

It's about the audience taking action.

1. With my game-changing facts, I'll challenge your thinking.

2. I share my personal experiences ... as well as a few stories from my time at Apple.

3. I demonstrate to the audience how to easily complete their goals and tasks on time.

4. You can bundle the speaking event to kick off a group Accountability coaching program for your team(s). Small groups of three to seven are ideal.

Read my other business book
The Accountability Advantage: Play your best game

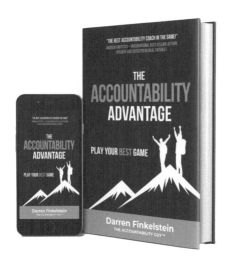

Introducing a simple, game-changing, 7-step road to accountability process that is easy to follow ...

- ☒ Increase the probability of achieving your goals to 95%.
- ☒ When you become truly accountable, the results change your life and business forever.
- ☒ Available in paperback and ebook formats.

Special voucher code: When ordering a copy of my book from my website, please use the special VIP discount/voucher code take50 at checkout in your cart to get a whopping 50% discount off the RRP with my compliments.

Take my 30-DAY Accountability Challenge

Wouldn't it be satisfying to finally finish that important task you've been putting off for ages?

Here's how to tick off any task on your To-Do List in the next 30 days (or sooner) without working harder, without letting anyone down and especially without giving up anything you love doing ...

Dear goal-kicker,

You know that important task that keeps getting bumped down your To-Do List by urgent busy-work?

The 30-Day Accountability Challenge will help you get it done so you can get on to the next exciting phase in your business or life. The process is really simple ...

1   First, I'll help you get **CLARITY** on what a successful outcome will look like.
2   Next, you'll make it a **PRIORITY** by coupling your goal to why it really matters.
3   Finally, we'll figure out what **ACTIVITY** needs to be done, when you will do it and who needs to be involved to make it possible.

How much more time, money and opportunity are you going to waste by putting it off?

In just a few weeks or days, you could be enjoying the relief, satisfaction and pride of finally having it done.

All you need is a helping hand from the best account-ability coach in the business ...

Game-changing facts to unlock your full potential

Did you know that a 2010 study by the American Society of Training and Development (ASTD) revealed the key factors that influence your probability of accomplishing a goal, task or project?

Here's the eye-opening breakdown:

- ☒ 10% chance of success if you merely have an idea or goal.
- ☒ 25% chance if you consciously decide to pursue it.
- ☒ 40% chance if you set a specific timeline.
- ☒ 50% chance if you create a detailed plan.
- ☒ 65% chance if you commit to someone else.
- ☒ A staggering 95% chance if you have a specific accountability appointment with the person you've committed to.

So, ask yourself this:

Can you truly achieve your goals, promises, obligations and commitments on your own?

The answer is clear – success is rarely a solo endeavour.

Embrace the power of accountability and unlock your full potential today! Why is this the case you say?

Good question. And the answer is because your capacity to say 'NO' more skilfully can be greatly enhanced by working with an accountability coach. This will help you focus on what's important and avoid distractions. Clarifying your priorities and goals is crucial to determining which chores are required and which are not, and this is something that an accountability coach can assist you with. It is simpler to decline offers or requests that don't fit with your objectives when they are clear.

A strategic plan that is customised to your goals is developed with the help of coaches. This plan makes it easier to distinguish between important duties and possible distractions by outlining the steps you need to take to accomplish your goals and assisting you in identifying the critical actions you need to do. When you have a well-defined plan, you can safely turn down anything that will not help you get closer to your objectives.

Working with a coach is also essential for developing self-discipline. Frequent progress reports and check-ins support you in staying committed to your objectives. Your ability to say 'NO' to unimportant chores will be strengthened by your greater discipline as you become more conscious of how your actions advance or hinder your goals.

Accountability coaching includes instruction on how to establish and uphold sound limits. These constraints relate to how you manage your own time and personal boundaries in addition to how you interact with other people. Establishing clear limits is crucial for efficiently handling requests for your time and attention, which in turn facilitates the ability to say 'NO' when it's needed.

Having an accountability coach's assistance increases your self-assurance in your capacity to make decisions. Refusing requests without feeling guilty is more likely to happen when you have confidence in your decision-making. Saying 'NO' is a powerful decision for both professional and personal growth, and coaches frequently emphasise this point. They also work on helping clients develop self-esteem.

Saying 'NO' can be tough for many people because they are afraid of missing out or worry about disappointing other people. Coaches offer positive coping mechanisms to assist you handle these emotions. With this assistance, you are able to make choices that are driven by your own interests rather than by fear or duty.

Besides all that, an accountability coach teaches you the value of time and efficient time-management techniques. This can entail figuring out which chores you can assign to others or take off entirely from your schedule. Saying 'NO' to activities that are not a good use of your time is crucial, and learning how to optimise your time emphasises this point.

Coaches assist you in staying focused on long-term goals rather than allowing yourself to become attached to instant satisfaction. Having a long-term perspective is essential to realising the effects of your decisions and recognising that certain seemingly good short-term chances could not be good long-term investments.

Working with an accountability coach improves your capacity to say 'NO' by encouraging a goal-oriented, disciplined approach, teaching you how to set reasonable limits, boosting your confidence in your ability to make decisions, and assisting you in controlling the feelings that come with rejection. This targeted strategy not only frees up your time and energy for the most crucial tasks, but also helps you to keep your everyday activities in line with your long-term goals for your work and personal life.

If you're looking for an accountability coach to work with you to get to that 95% probability of hitting your goals, tasks and commitments, then why not engage me?

After all, here's what Andrew Griffiths and Callum Laing have to say about my coaching programs and my ability to deliver outcomes:

'The best accountability coach in the game.'

Andrew Griffiths – international bestselling author and speaker

'One of the world's leading accountability coaches.'

Callum Laing – investor/entrepreneur, Veblen Director Programme

About Darren Finkelstein

Darren Finkelstein, known widely as The Accountability Guy®, is a beacon of transformation and inspiration in the realms of accountability, leadership and personal development. Darren's story is about resilience, reinvention and how he's channelled accountability into his superpower.

With a career that spans continents and industries, Darren stands as a formidable international accountability coach, advisor, mentor and captivating author and speaker whose methodologies have empowered high-performing individuals and teams from Australia and New Zealand to the far reaches of Latin America, Europe, Asia, the United Kingdom and the United States through his coaching programs.

Darren's methodology and teachings are based around his bestselling books, *The Accountability Advantage: Play your best game* and *NO: Building a life of choice without obligation*. Darren's focus is to help his clients to Get Clarity: Know what to do FIRST, Get Started: Know what to do NEXT, and Get Stuff Done: Know what to do MORE of. Darren works with high-performing individuals and teams to help them realise their wildest dreams and smash their goals like glass piñatas!

Before etching his name in the annals of coaching and mentorship, Darren was an integral part of the Apple legacy during the transformative Steve Jobs era. As the Manager of Commercial Markets for Apple Australia, his innovations, sales performance and leadership were recognised with the prestigious 'Golden Apple' Award for Asia Pacific, symbolising his influence in shaping the future of technology and business strategy. His journey from the suburbs of Melbourne to the upper echelons of Silicon Valley embodies a story of relentless ambition and the pursuit of dreams against the odds.

Post-Apple, Darren embarked on a genuine 'sea change', transitioning from the tech giant to co-founding a boutique lifestyle business in the marine industry alongside business partner Andrew Rose, which they successfully sold and exited to follow their own dreams.

This venture not only scaled new heights but also led Darren to become a major figure in the marine community. His literary contributions – the bestselling and much-publicised trilogy *Honey, Let's Buy a BOAT!*, *Honey, Let's Go BOATING!* and *Honey, Let's Sell the BOAT!* – further cemented his status as an industry luminary and a visionary thinker.

Darren's voice resonated beyond the printed page and into the Melbourne airwaves as a seasoned radio presenter on 3AW, where he delivered the engaging Beach 'N' Bay reports, blending his passion for the outdoors with his expertise in lifestyle and the marine environment.

His entrepreneurial journey continued to flourish with accolades such as the 'Entrepreneur of the Year' award from the Dent Global 'Key Person of Influence' program, where he currently serves as a Dent Coach, nurturing the next generation of business leaders.

Despite his vast professional achievements, Darren's heart beats for the simple joy of golf and working on his small farm, embodying his philosophy of embracing life's challenges with enthusiasm and resilience, even if it means struggling to hit them straight on the golf course with consistency.

Darren Finkelstein's story not only teaches us about achieving the pinnacle of success, but also imparts lessons about resilience and reinvention. He inspires change, transforms concepts into reality, and assists others in creating extraordinary narratives by channelling their passions and dreams.

Darren often says to his family, *'What you imagine, you create; now let's get going.'*

With Darren by your side and in your corner as your coach, advisor and mentor, the road to accountability and beyond is not just a route but a magnificent trip that is just waiting to be discovered.

Find out more about Darren here

Join Darren on socials

Facebook – follow

Instagram – follow

LinkedIn – connect

YouTube – subscribe

Google My Business – leave a review

Contact

Mobile: +61 418 379 369
Email: df@tickthoseboxes.com.au

JASDN Family Trust
trading as:
Tick Those Boxes Australia and Suzi Finkelstein Advisory
P.O. Box 282
Caulfield South 3162
Victoria. Australia
ABN: 21 103 787 352

Important stuff you must understand

Disclaimer (and the not-so-fine print)

General advice warning

The content of *NO: Building a life of choice without obligation* ('the book'), including but not limited to opinions, advice, tips, suggestions and recommendations, is for general information purposes only and does not take into account your specific circumstances. Darren Finkelstein ('the author') and the publisher are not providing professional, legal or financial advice through the book.

The author and the publisher make no representations or warranties of any kind, express or implied, about the completeness, accuracy, reliability, suitability or availability with respect to the book or the information contained on its pages for any purpose. Any reliance you place on such information is, therefore, strictly at your own risk.

In no event will the author or the publisher be liable for any loss or damage, including, without limitation, indirect or consequential loss or damage, or any loss or damage whatsoever arising from loss of data or profits arising out of, or in connection with, the use of this book.

Before making any decision or taking any action, you should consult a professional who can advise you based on your own individual situation. This is especially important for financial decisions, as the book does not provide personalised financial advice.

Neither Darren Finkelstein nor the publisher are licensed financial advisers, nor are they lawyers, accountants, medical professionals and/or marriage counsellors. Author Darren Finkelstein's personal experiences and subject matter research are the only sources of material used for the creation of this publication.

Financial advice in Australia

In Australia, giving financial advice is regulated by the Australian Securities and Investments Commission (ASIC). Financial advice must be given by an individual or an entity that holds an Australian Financial Services Licence (AFSL). It is illegal to provide financial advice or recommend financial products to others in Australia without the appropriate licence or authority.

If you are seeking financial advice, it is important to ensure that the adviser is licenced and qualified to provide the advice. Always verify the credentials of a financial adviser and confirm they are registered with ASIC.

Indemnification

By using the information provided in the book, you agree to indemnify, defend and hold harmless the author and the publisher from any claims, damages, losses, liabilities, and all costs and expenses of defence, including but not limited to, attorneys' fees, resulting directly or indirectly from a claim by a third party that is based on your use of the book in violation of these terms.

Jurisdiction

This disclaimer is governed by the laws of Australia and shall be subject to the exclusive jurisdiction of the courts of Australia.

Notes

Notes

Notes

Notes

Notes